C000022636

Scotl

CARAVAN AND CAMPING 2008

Published by VisitScotland, 2007 Photography Paul Tomkins / VisitScotland / Scottish Viewpoint www.visitscotland.com 0845 22 55 121

Plockton, looking across Loch Carron towards Applecross, Highlands

WELCOME TO SCOTLAND

Once you've enjoyed a holiday in Scotland, it is easy to see why so many people from all over the world visit time and again. Scotland is a wonderful place for holidaymakers. From the briefest of breaks to annual vacations, Scotland has so much to offer that you'll never run out of options.

Flick through the pages of this guide and you'll immediately get a flavour of Scotland's diversity. You'll discover an inspiring array of fascinating places, each with its own unique attractions.

The best small country in the world

Though it's a relatively small country, Scotland is remarkably varied. You can climb mountains in the morning and still be on the beach in the afternoon. You can canoe across a remote loch and never see another soul all day long or you can sip coffee in a city centre pavement café and watch the whole world go by. You can get dressed up to the nines and go to a world premier on a balmy summer's evening or you can join in with some traditional folk songs round a welcoming log fire in a quaint little pub on a cold winter's night.

Because of its remarkable diversity, Scotland is a world-class holiday destination all year round. There's always something happening, and when you get to where you're going, you'll be spoiled for choice for somewhere to stay.

Get out and explore

When you're camping or caravanning, you can also get close to nature and explore a wilder side of Scotland. Though many of Scotland's caravan sites are now very sophisticated with a wide range of home comforts, others have retained that degree of simplicity that makes camping and caravanning so enjoyable.

So if it's adventure you're looking for, this is the way to go. With your tent on your back or your mobile home at your disposal, you're free to tour around and explore. There's an excellent range of holiday parks and sites all over the country – often in quite stunning locations. You can also enjoy the benefits of a caravan holiday without doing any of the towing yourself as many parks provide caravans for hire.

So whether you're planning to visit one of the larger parks or somewhere much more remote, you'll be able to look forward to a rousing welcome in a country that is renowned for its hospitality.

Great times await

Nobody loves a good time like the Scots. Whether it's bringing in the New Year with a wee dram, swirling your partner at a ceilidh or enjoying a delightful dinner for two in an exclusive restaurant with a stunning view, unforgettable experiences are never far away.

There's always the chance too that you'll meet some great folks – locals and other visitors – some of whom could well become friends for life. That's all just part of a visit to Scotland. As they say in the Gaelic tongue, *ceud mille failte* – 'a hundred thousand welcomes'. Come and enjoy our beautiful country.

Loch Awe and Kilchurn Castle, Argyll

Top left: A group of walkers near Glen Doll and Glen Clova, Angus   Top right: Puffins on the Isle of Staffa, Inner Hebrides
Bottom: West Sands Beach, St Andrews, Fife

DON'T MISS

Walking

From the rolling hills in the south to the Angus Glens, to the mountainous north, Scotland is perfect for walkers whether it's a gentle stroll or a serious trek.

Beaches

Scotland's beaches are something special whether it's for a romantic stroll, or to try some surfing. Explore Fife's Blue Flag beaches or the breathtaking beaches in the Outer Hebrides.

Wildlife

From dolphins in the Moray Firth to capercaillie in the Highlands and seals and puffins on the coastline, you never know what you might spot.

Culture & Heritage

From the mysterious standing stones in Orkney and the Outer Hebrides to Burns Cottage and Rosslyn Chapel, traces of Scotland's history are never hard to find.

Ring of Brodgar, Orkney

Adventure

From rock climbing to white water rafting, you can do it all. Try Perthshire for some unusual adventure activities or the south of Scotland for some serious mountain biking.

Mountain biking in Glentress Forest, Scottish Borders

Shopping

From designer stores to unique boutiques, from Glasgow's swanky city centre to Edinburgh's eclectic Old Town, Scotland is a shopper's paradise with lots of hidden gems to uncover.

Victoria Street, Edinburgh

Golf

The country that gave the world the game of golf is still the best place to play it. Why not check out the historic courses in Ayrshire or Angus.

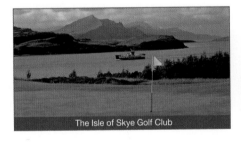
The Isle of Skye Golf Club

Castles

Wherever you are in Scotland you are never far from a great Scottish icon whether it's an impressive ruin or an imposing fortress, a fairytale castle or country estate.

Caerlaverock Castle, Dumfries and Galloway

Highland Games

From the famous Braemar Gathering in Aberdeenshire to the spectacular Cowal Highland Gathering in Argyll, hot foot it to a Highland Games for pipe bands, dancers, and tossing the caber.

Ballater Highland Games, Aberdeenshire

Events & Festivals

In Scotland there's so much going on with fabulous events and festivals throughout the year, wherever you choose to visit, from the biggest names to the quirky and traditional.

The Royal Mile during the Festival, Edinburgh

If you love food, get a taste of Scotland. A climate without extremes and the unspoilt environment provide the ideal conditions so Scotland's natural larder offers some of the best produce in the world. Scotland's coastal waters are home to an abundance of lobster, prawns, oysters and more, whilst the land produces world famous beef, lamb and game.

There's high quality food and drink on menus all over the country often cooked up by award-winning chefs in restaurants where the view is second to none. You'll find home cooking, fine dining, takeaways and tearooms. Whether you're looking for a family-friendly pub or a romantic Highland restaurant there's the perfect place to dine. And there's no better time to indulge than when you're on holiday!

Traditional fare

Haggis and whisky might be recognised as traditional Scottish fare but why not add cullen skink, clapshot, cranachan, and clootie dumpling to the list...discover the tastes that match such ancient names. Sample some local hospitality along with regional specialities such as the Selkirk Bannock or Arbroath Smokies. Or experience the freedom of eating fish and chips straight from the wrapper while breathing in the clear evening air.

Farmers' markets

Scotland is a land renowned for producing ingredients of the highest quality. You can handpick fresh local produce at farmers' markets in towns and cities across the country. Create your own culinary delights or learn from the masters at the world famous Nick Nairn Cook School in Stirling. Savour the aroma, excite your taste buds and experience the buzz of a farmers' market.

EATING AND DRINKING

Events

Scotland serves up a full calendar of food and drink festivals. Events like Taste of Edinburgh and Highland Feast are a must for foodies. Whisky fans can share their passion at the Islay Malt Whisky Festival, the Highland Whisky Festival, or the Spirit of Speyside Whisky Festival.

Tours and trails

If you're a lover of seafood spend some time exploring the rugged, unspoilt coastline of mid-Argyll following The Seafood Trail. Or if you fancy a wee dram visit the eight distilleries and cooperage on the world's only Malt Whisky Trail in Speyside. Look out for the new Scottish Café Trail for Scotland's best café experiences, and enjoy a cup of something lovely surrounded by amazing scenery.

EatScotland

EatScotland is a nationwide Quality Assurance Scheme from VisitScotland. The scheme includes all sectors of the catering industry from chip shops, pubs and takeaways to restaurants. A trained team of assessors carry out an incognito visit to assess quality, standards and ambience. Only those operators who meet the EatScotland quality standards are accredited to the scheme so look out for the logo to ensure you visit Scotland's best quality establishments.

The newly launched EatScotland Silver and Gold Award Scheme recognises outstanding standards, reflecting that an establishment offers an excellent eating out experience in Scotland.

www.eatscotland.com

Al fresco dining, Edinburgh

GREEN TOURISM

THE Green Tourism BUSINESS SCHEME
SILVER

Scotland is a stunning destination and we want to make sure it stays that way. That's why we encourage all tourism operators including accommodation providers to take part in our Green Tourism Business Scheme. It means you're assured of a great quality stay at an establishment that's trying to minimise its impact on the environment.

VisitScotland rigorously assesses accommodation providers against measures as diverse as energy use, using local produce on menus, or promoting local wildlife walks or cycle hire. Environmentally responsible businesses can achieve Bronze, Silver or Gold awards, to acknowledge how much they are doing to help conserve the quality of Scotland's beautiful environment.

Look out for the Bronze, Silver and Gold Green Tourism logos throughout this guide to help you decide where to stay and do your bit to help protect our environment.

www.green-business.co.uk

Bronze
Green Tourism Award

Silver
Green Tourism Award

Gold
Green Tourism Award

Friendly and knowledgeable staff are able to answer your questions and give advice

TOURIST INFORMATION

Make the most of your stay in Scotland and call into a Tourist Information Centre wherever you go.

- There are over 100 Tourist Information Centres across Scotland.
- Knowledgeable and friendly staff are there to answer questions, give advice, and turn a good holiday into an unforgettable experience.
- Tell the staff what you're interested in doing and they'll suggest the best places to go.
- Staff can help you find and book accommodation anywhere in Scotland.
- Each centre has a wide stock of free guides and leaflets featuring local attractions and places of interest.
- Each centre also has an excellent range of maps, guide books, Scottish literature and books that you can buy.
- You can buy tickets for local and national events and book excursions, tours and travel.
- Most offer a splendid range of souvenirs and local crafts which make ideal gifts for you to take home for friends and family.
- Some centres also provide a bureau de change service and internet access.

VisitScotland, under the Scottish Tourist Board brand, administers the star grading schemes which assess the quality and standards of all types of tourist accommodation and visitor attractions from castles and historic houses to garden centres and arts venues. We grade around 80 per cent of the accommodation in Scotland and 90 per cent of the visitor attractions - so wherever you want to stay or visit, we've got it covered. The schemes are monitored all year round and reviewed once a year. We do the hard work so you can relax and enjoy your holiday.

The promise of the stars:

★
It is clean, tidy and an acceptable, if basic, standard

★★
It is a good, all round standard

★★★
It is a very good standard, with attention to detail in every area

★★★★
It is excellent – using high quality materials, good food (except self-catering) and friendly, professional service

★★★★★
An exceptional standard where presentation, ambience, food (except self-catering) and service are hard to fault.

IT'S WRITTEN IN THE STARS...

How does the system work?

Our advisors visit and assess establishments on up to 50 areas from quality, comfort and cleanliness to welcome, ambience and service. If an establishment scores less than 60 per cent it will not be graded. The same star scheme now runs in England and Wales, so you can follow the stars wherever you go.

Graded visitor attractions

Visitor attractions from castles and museums to leisure centres and tours are graded with 1-5 stars depending on their level of customer care. The focus is on the standard of hospitality and service as well as presentation, quality of shop or café (if there is one) and toilet facilities.

 This means that a bothy or bod has been inspected.

 The Thistle symbol recognises a high standard of caravan holiday home.

 This means individual caravan holiday homes have been inspected.

We want you to feel welcome

Walkers Welcome and Cyclists Welcome. Establishments that carry the symbols below pay particular attention to the specific needs of walkers and cyclists.

 Cyclists Welcome

 Walkers Welcome

There are similar schemes for Anglers, Bikers, Classic Cars, Golfers, Children and Ancestral Tourism. Check with establishment when booking.

Access all areas

The following symbols will help visitors with physical disabilities to decide whether accommodation is suitable.

 Unassisted wheelchair access

 Assisted wheelchair access

 Access for visitors with mobility difficulties

The Glenfinnan Viaduct, Highlands

TRAVEL TO SCOTLAND

It's really easy to get to Scotland whether you choose to travel by car, train, plane, coach or ferry. And once you get here travel is easy as Scotland is a compact country.

By Air

Flying to Scotland couldn't be simpler with flight times from London, Dublin and Belfast only around one hour. There are airports at Edinburgh, Glasgow, Glasgow Prestwick, Aberdeen, Dundee and Inverness. The following airlines operate flights to Scotland (although not all airports) from within the UK and Ireland:

bmi
Tel: 0870 60 70 555
From Ireland: 1332 64 8181
flybmi.com

bmi baby
Tel: 0871 224 0224
From Ireland: 1 890 340 122
bmibaby.com

British Airways
Tel: 0870 850 9 850
From Ireland: 1890 626 747
ba.com

Eastern Airways
Tel: 08703 669 100
easternairways.com

easyJet
Tel: 0905 821 0905
From Ireland: 1890 923 922
easyjet.com

Flybe
Tel: 0871 522 6100
From Ireland: 1392 268 529
flybe.com

Ryanair
Tel: 0871 246 0000
From Ireland: 0818 30 30 30
ryanair.com

Air France
Tel: 0870 142 4343
airfrance.co.uk

Aer Arann
Tel: 0870 876 76 76
From Ireland: 0818 210 210
aerarann.com

Jet2
Tel: 0871 226 1737
From Ireland: 0818 200017
jet2.com

AirBerlin
Tel: 0871 5000 737
airberlin.com

Aer Lingus
Tel: 0870 876 5000
From Ireland: 0818 365 000
aerlingus.com

By Rail

Scotland has major rail stations in Aberdeen, Edinburgh Waverley and Edinburgh Haymarket, Glasgow Queen Street and Glasgow Central, Perth, Stirling, Dundee and Inverness. There are regular cross border railway services from England and Wales, and good city links. You could even travel on the First ScotRail Caledonian Sleeper overnight train service from London and wake up to the sights and sounds of Scotland.

First ScotRail
Tel: 08457 55 00 33
firstscotrail.com

Virgin Trains
Tel: 08457 222 333
virgintrains.co.uk

GNER
Tel: 08457 225 225
gner.co.uk

By Road

Scotland has an excellent road network from motorways and dual carriageway linking cities and major towns, to remote single-track roads with passing places to let others by. Whether you are coming in your own car from home or hiring a car once you get here, getting away from traffic jams and out onto Scotland's quiet roads can really put the fun back into driving. Branches of the following companies can be found throughout Scotland:

Arnold Clark
Tel: 0845 702 3946
arnoldclark.com/rental

easyCar
Tel: 0906 333 3333
easycar.com

Hertz
Tel: 08708 44 88 44
hertz.co.uk

Avis Rent A Car
Tel: 0870 606 0100
avis.co.uk

Enterprise Rent-A-Car
Tel: 0870 350 3000
enterprise.co.uk

National Car Rental
Tel: 0870 400 4560
nationalcar.com

Budget
Tel: 08701 56 56 56
budget.co.uk

Europcar
Tel: 0870 607 5000
europcarscotland.co.uk

Sixt rent a car
Tel: 0870 156 7567
sixt.co.uk

By Ferry

Scotland has over 130 inhabited islands so ferries are important. And whether you are coming from Ireland or trying to get to the outer islands, you might be in need of a ferry crossing. Ferries to and around the islands are regular and reliable and most carry vehicles. These companies all operate ferry services around Scotland:

Stena Line
Tel: 08705 204 204
stenaline.co.uk

Caledonian MacBrayne
Tel: 08705 650000
calmac.co.uk

Northlink Ferries
Tel: 08456 000 449
northlinkferries.co.uk

P&O Irish Sea
Tel: 0870 24 24 777
poirishsea.com

Western Ferries
Tel: 01369 704 452
western-ferries.co.uk

By Coach

Coach connections include express services to Scotland from all over the UK, and there is a good network of coach services once you get here too. You could even travel on the Postbus – a special feature of the Scottish mail service which carries fare-paying passengers along with the mail in rural areas where there is no other form of transport, bringing a new dimension to travel.

National Express
Tel: 08705 80 80 80
nationalexpress.com

City Link
Tel: 08705 50 50 50
citylink.co.uk

Postbus
Tel: 08457 740 740
royalmail.com/postbus

DRIVING DISTANCES

Driving distances chart (upper number = miles (M), lower number = kilometres (KM)).

To \ From	ABERDEEN	BIRMINGHAM	CARDIFF	DOVER	DUMFRIES	DUNDEE	EDINBURGH	FORT WILLIAM	GLASGOW	HARWICH	HULL	INVERNESS	KYLE OF LOCHALSH	LONDON	MANCHESTER	NEWCASTLE	OBAN	PERTH	PRESTWICK	ROSYTH	STIRLING	STRANRAER	THURSO	TROON	ULLAPOOL
BIRMINGHAM	421/687																								
CARDIFF	529/851	113/182																							
DOVER	617/993	200/322	224/361																						
DUMFRIES	214/344	234/376	335/539	436/700																					
DUNDEE	71/114	357/575	465/749	553/890	149/240																				
EDINBURGH	131/210	290/467	398/641	486/782	80/128	62/99																			
FORT WILLIAM	161/258	396/637	504/811	592/952	179/288	123/197	138/221																		
GLASGOW	152/243	286/461	394/634	482/776	76/122	84/134	45/72	108/173																	
HARWICH	604/972	187/300	242/390	130/210	370/595	540/869	473/761	578/931	469/754																
HULL	178/287	243/391	344/554	417/671	53/86	113/182	50/81	185/298	85/137	370/596															
INVERNESS	387/619	137/221	251/405	255/411	205/330	318/509	255/408	384/614	275/440	214/346	206/331														
KYLE OF LOCHALSH	118/189	446/717	553/890	641/1032	239/385	134/214	162/259	69/110	178/285	628/1011	209/337	444/710													
LONDON	549/878	118/190	150/242	75/122	349/561	481/770	412/659	514/822	406/650	78/126	358/576	216/346	573/917												
MANCHESTER	345/556	93/150	201/324	281/453	157/252	281/453	214/345	320/515	210/338	268/431	166/267	95/154	370/595	201/322											
NEWCASTLE	244/390	208/336	323/519	350/563	91/147	175/280	112/179	267/427	159/254	309/498	64/102	148/237	274/438	288/461	147/237										
OBAN	190/304	385/620	493/794	581/935	168/270	121/194	125/200	50/80	96/154	568/914	175/281	371/594	112/180	502/803	309/498	310/496									
PERTH	86/139	348/560	449/723	550/884	128/205	21/34	43/69	104/166	64/104	484/778	96/155	319/513	114/183	436/744	271/436	152/245	94/151								
PRESTWICK	177/285	304/489	411/662	500/804	61/98	113/182	79/127	127/204	21/34	430/692	105/168	279/449	201/324	418/673	228/366	168/271	120/193	96/155							
ROSYTH	115/185	324/522	425/684	477/768	104/170	48/77	14/23	124/200	47/76	486/783	67/108	265/426	145/233	437/703	247/398	183/198	123/198	31/49	79/127						
STIRLING	120/193	313/503	414/666	514/823	92/149	55/89	38/61	97/157	29/47	448/722	87/142	284/456	145/234	427/688	236/379	143/231	114/183	37/60	60/54	26/42					
STRANRAER	241/386	297/478	404/651	489/787	71/115	172/275	133/213	196/314	89/142	475/765	125/202	284/454	234/435	415/664	224/358	161/259	149/240	172/277	54/87	131/211	114/183				
THURSO	234/374	555/893	663/1066	750/1208	348/560	250/400	278/445	183/293	293/469	737/1186	424/765	177/283	435/690	690/1104	358/626	259/391	277/626	240/373	373/311	221/500	373/409	406/382	183/508		
TROON	183/295	314/505	415/668	516/830	64/104	126/203	35/56	56/450	209/35	724/171	106/171	285/459	265/504	209/429	336/237	200/381	116/186	101/221	5/8	162/101	129/80	63/101	96/316	60/327	
ULLAPOOL	179/286	499/803	607/976	695/1118	293/472	194/310	222/355	119/190	238/381	681/1097	263/424	91/146	63/101	635/1016	444/710	335/536	169/270	199/320	128/205	199/237	320/270	370/382	128/226	205/363	231/372
YORK	343/552	132/212	246/396	273/439	151/243	279/449	191/308	318/511	208/335	233/374	152/245	41/65	367/591	391/630	208/335	70/113	90/146	307/495	237/382	226/363	212/341	230/370	477/767	218/352	231/372

M = miles   KM = kilometres

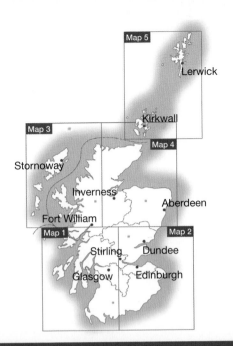

MAPS

MAP 1

MAP 2

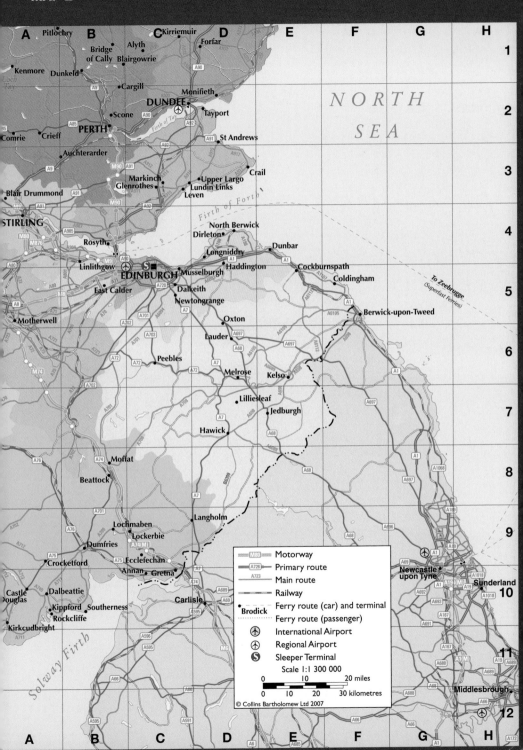

NORTH SEA

To Zeebrugge (Superfast Ferries)

Pitlochry, Kirriemuir, Forfar, Bridge of Cally, Alyth, Blairgowrie, Kenmore, Dunkeld, Cargill, Monifieth, Comrie, Crieff, Scone, Tayport, **PERTH**, **DUNDEE**, Auchterarder, St Andrews, Blair Drummond, Markinch, Glenrothes, Upper Largo, Crail, Lundin Links, Leven, **STIRLING**, Rosyth, North Berwick, Dirleton, Dunbar, Linlithgow, Longniddry, Cockburnspath, East Calder, **EDINBURGH**, Musselburgh, Haddington, Coldingham, Motherwell, Dalkeith, Newtongrange, Oxton, Berwick-upon-Tweed, Lauder, Peebles, Melrose, Kelso, Moffat, Lilliesleaf, Beattock, Jedburgh, Hawick, Langholm, Lochmaben, Lockerbie, Newcastle upon Tyne, Dumfries, Ecclefechan, Sunderland, Crocketford, Annan, Gretna, Castle Douglas, Carlisle, Dalbeattie, Kippford, Southerness, Rockcliffe, Kirkcudbright, Middlesbrough

Loch Tay
Firth of Tay
Firth of Forth
Solway Firth

Legend

M80	Motorway
A726	Primary route
A723	Main route
	Railway
	Ferry route (car) and terminal
Brodick	Ferry route (passenger)
✈	International Airport
✈	Regional Airport
Ⓢ	Sleeper Terminal

Scale 1:1 300 000

0   10   20 miles
0   10   20   30 kilometres

© Collins Bartholomew Ltd 2007

MAP 3

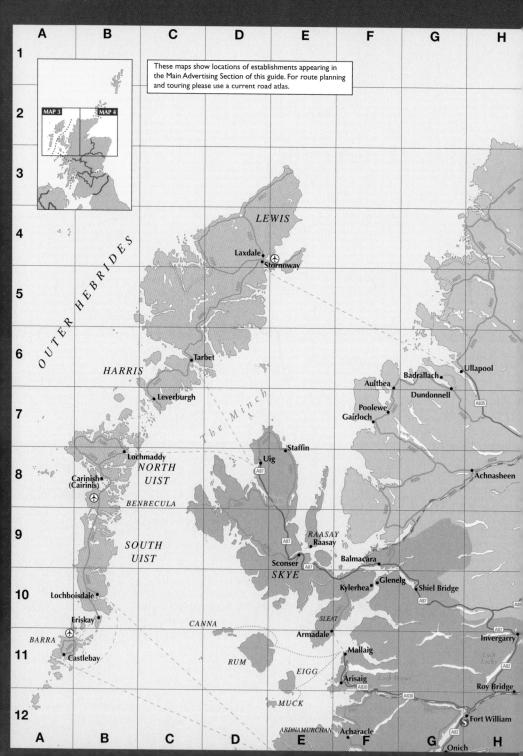

These maps show locations of establishments appearing in the Main Advertising Section of this guide. For route planning and touring please use a current road atlas.

MAP 3

MAP 4

OUTER HEBRIDES

LEWIS

Laxdale
Stornoway

HARRIS

Tarbet

Leverburgh

The Minch

Lochmaddy

Carinish
(Cairinis)

NORTH UIST

BENBECULA

SOUTH UIST

Uig
Staffin

A87

RAASAY
Raasay

Sconser
SKYE

A87

Lochboisdale

Eriskay

BARRA

Castlebay

CANNA

RUM

SLEAT

Armadale

EIGG

MUCK

ARDNAMURCHAN

Acharacle

Aultbea
Badrallach
Ullapool
Dundonnell
A835

Poolewe
Gairloch

Achnasheen

Balmacara

Kylerhea
Glenelg
Shiel Bridge

A87

Mallaig

Arisaig
A830

A830

Invergarry

Roy Bridge

Fort William

Onich

MAP 4

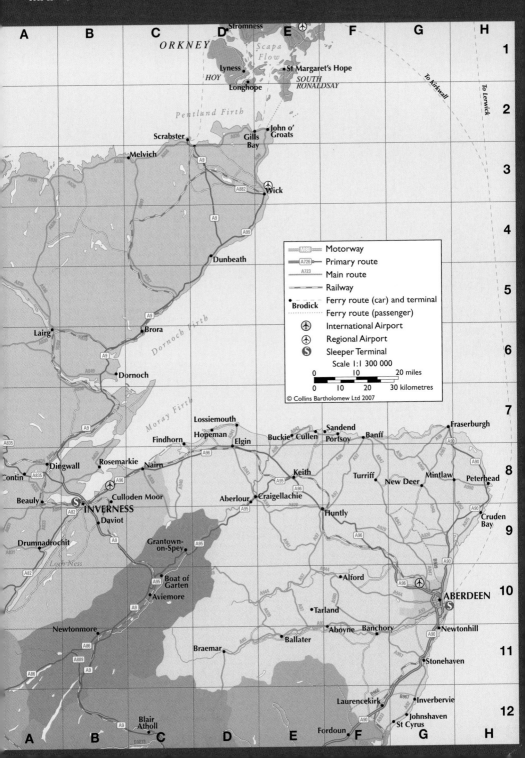

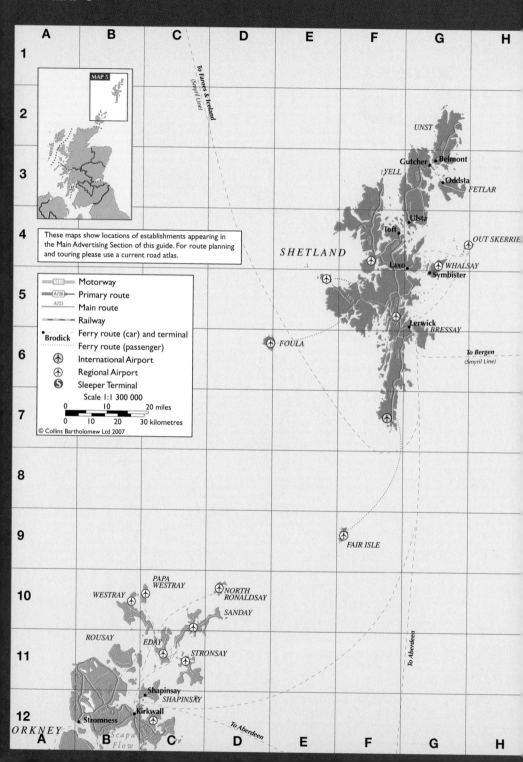

MAP 5

	A	B	C	D	E	F	G	H

MAP 5

These maps show locations of establishments appearing in the Main Advertising Section of this guide. For route planning and touring please use a current road atlas.

To Faroes & Iceland
(Smyril Line)

Motorway
M80

Primary route
A726

Main route
A723

Railway

Brodick
Ferry route (car) and terminal

Ferry route (passenger)

International Airport

Regional Airport

S Sleeper Terminal

Scale 1:1 300 000

0   10   20 miles
0 10 20 30 kilometres

© Collins Bartholomew Ltd 2007

UNST

Gutcher   Belmont

YELL   Oddsta

FETLAR

Ulsta

Toft

OUT SKERRIE

SHETLAND

Laxo   WHALSAY
Symbister

Lerwick
BRESSAY

To Bergen
(Smyril Line)

FOULA

FAIR ISLE

PAPA
WESTRAY

WESTRAY   NORTH
RONALDSAY

SANDAY

ROUSAY   EDAY

STRONSAY

To Aberdeen

Shapinsay
SHAPINSAY

Kirkwall

Stromness

ORKNEY

Scapa
Flow

To Aberdeen

Camping at Gairloch, Highlands

ACCOMMODATION LISTINGS

- Caravan and camping **accommodation listings** for all of Scotland.

- Establishments are listed **by location** in alphabetical order.

- At the back of the book there is a listing of **Accessible Accommodation** for visitors with mobility difficulties.

- For a full listing of all VisitScotland quality assured caravan and camping accommodation see the **Directory** at the back.

- You will also find an **Index by location** which will tell you where to look if you already know where you want to go.

- Inside the back cover flap you will find a **key to the symbols**.

Kirriereoch Loch in Galloway Forest Park, Dumfries & Galloway

SOUTH OF SCOTLAND

Ayrshire & Arran,
Dumfries & Galloway,
Scottish Borders

No matter how many times you holiday in the Scottish Borders, Ayrshire & Arran or Dumfries & Galloway, you'll always find something new and interesting to do.

The proud heritage, distinct traditions and enthralling history of Scotland's most southerly places are sure to capture your imagination.

Across the south, the trail of an often bloody and turbulent past is easily followed from imposing castles to ruined abbeys. It's a story of battles and skirmishes from all out war to cattle rustling cross-border raids.

Living history

Though you'd be hard pushed to find a more peaceful part of the country these days, the legacy of these more unsettled times can still be experienced in many a Border town during the Common Ridings. Throughout the summer months hundreds of colourful riders on horseback commemorate the days when their ancestors risked their lives patrolling town boundaries and neighbouring villages.

The south is alive with history. Traquair House, near Innerleithen, is Scotland's oldest continuously inhabited house, dating back to 1107. In Selkirk the whole town is transformed in early December as locals step back to the days when Sir Walter Scott presided over the local courtroom, by partaking in the Scott's Selkirk celebrations.

Beautiful beaches

Southern Scotland isn't just about rolling hills and lush farmland, both coasts are well worth a visit. To the east you can see the rocky cliffs and picturesque harbours at St Abbs Head and Eyemouth, while over on the west, there are the beautiful Ayrshire beaches and more than 200 miles of the lovely Solway Coast to explore.

And off the Ayrshire coast is the Isle of Arran – one of Scotland's finest islands and everything a holidaymaker could want.

And in many ways that sums up all of southern Scotland. Whatever you like doing, you'll be spoiled for choice. So, for example, if you love angling, there's world-class salmon fishing on the Tweed. If golf's your game, Turnberry, Prestwick and Royal Troon are up with the best.

If you're a mountain biker, you won't find better than Glentress, one of the 7stanes mountain bike routes. Enjoy reading? Head for Wigtown, Scotland's National Book Town and home to more than 20 bookshops. Ice cream? Who can resist Cream o' Galloway at Gatehouse of Fleet?

If you're a gardener, you'll be inspired all year round by the flourishing collection of rare plants at the Logan Botanic Garden near Stranraer and Dawyck Botanic Garden near Peebles.

That's the South of Scotland. Bursting with brilliant places, including some excellent parks for caravanning and camping, and waiting with a hearty Scottish welcome that will provide you with a holiday experience you will never forget.

Galashiels Braw Lads' Gathering, Scottish Borders

What's On?

Easter in the Borders
23 March 2008
Events at Floors Castle, Traquair House, Paxton House, and Thirlestane Castle.

125th Melrose 7's Rugby Tournament
11 – 13 April 2008
www.melrose7s.com

burns an' a' that! Festival, Ayrshire
May 2008 (dates tbc)
www.visitscotland.com/burns

Newton Stewart Walking Festival
9 – 15 May 2008
Biggest walking festival in the south.
www.newtonstewartwalkfest.co.uk

Arran Wildlife Festival
14 – 21 May 2008
www.arranwildlife.co.uk

Spring Fling, Dumfries & Galloway
24 – 26 May 2008
Open art and craft studios.
www.spring-fling.co.uk

Border Common Ridings
June – August 2008

Kirkcudbright Jazz Festival
12-15 June 2008
Jazz lovers flock to the town.
www.kirkcudbrightjazzfestival.co.uk

Borders Book Festival, Melrose
19 – 22 June 2008
www.bordersbookfestival.org

Marymass, Irvine
14 – 25 August 2008
www.marymass.org

Ayr Gold Cup Festival
18 -20 September 2008
www.ayr-racecourse.co.uk

The Hairth World Music Festival, Carsphairn
19 – 21 September 2008
Equinox world music festival.
www.knockengorroch.org.uk

www.ayrshire-arran.com
www.visitdumfriesandgalloway.co.uk
www.visitscottishborders.com

All dates correct at time of publication. Please check before booking. VisitScotland cannot be held responsible for any inaccuracies.

21

MAP

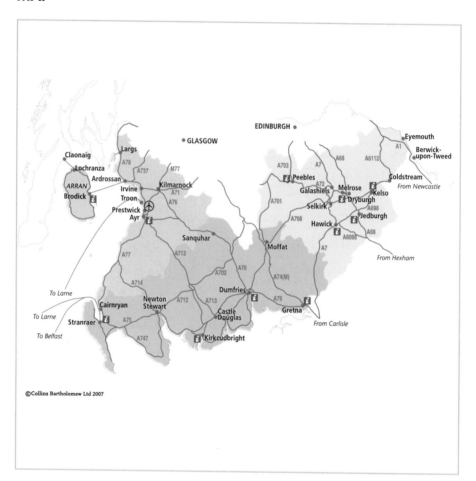

©Collins Bartholomew Ltd 2007

TOURIST INFORMATION CENTRES

Ayrshire & Arran	
Ayr	22 Sandgate, Ayr KA7 1BW
Brodick	The Pier, Brodick, Isle of Arran KA27 8AU

Dumfries & Galloway	
Dumfries	64 Whitesands, Dumfries DG1 2RS
Gretna	Unit 10, Gretna Gateway Outlet Village, Glasgow Road, Gretna DG16 5GG
Kirkcudbright	Harbour Square, Kirkcudbright DG6 4HY
Stranraer	Burns House, 28 Harbour Street, Stranraer, Dumfries DG9 7RA

Scottish Borders	
Hawick	Drumlanrig's Tower, Tower Knowe, Hawick TD9 9EN
Jedburgh	Murray's Green, Jedburgh TD8 6BE
Kelso	Town House, The Square, Kelso TD5 7HF
Melrose	Abbey House, Abbey Street, Melrose TD6 9LG
Peebles	23 High Street, Peebles EH45 8AG

Make the most of your stay in Scotland and make your first stop the Tourist Information Centre wherever you go.

Knowledgeable and friendly staff can help you with information and advice; they can answer your questions, book accommodation and you can even pick up some souvenirs to take home for friends and family.

For information and ideas about exploring Scotland in advance of your trip, call our booking and information service or go to **www.visitscotland.com**

Call 0845 22 55 121

or if calling from outside the UK call
+44 (0) 1506 832 121

From Ireland call
1800 932 510

A £4 booking fee applies to telephone bookings of accommodation.

Glen Rosa, Isle of Arran

Ayrshire & Arran

Lying to the south of Glasgow, Ayrshire is a beautiful part of the world characterised by rolling green hills inland and sandy beaches round the coast.

There are some great places to visit whether you're heading to Ayr for the horse racing, touring round the country villages or jumping on the ferry at Ardrossan and sailing for Arran.

The Isle of Arran is an enchanted world that seems to pack everything that makes Scotland great into a space that's just 19 miles from top to bottom and 10 miles at its widest. There's a castle, a distillery, rugged mountains to the north, gentle hills to the south, pretty towns and villages, beaches, wildlife, fishing and seven golf courses.

Ayrshire is also Burns Country and the footsteps of Scotland's greatest ever poet can be traced all round the south. Born in Alloway, South Ayrshire in 1759, you can now visit Robert Burns' birthplace and learn about his life and see the sights that inspired him at the Burns National Heritage Park.

Burns Cottage, Alloway, Ayrshire

DON'T MISS

1. See what happens when you bring four of the world's best graffiti artists to Scotland and provide them with a castle as a canvas. This is exactly what the owners of **Kelburn Castle** did. Kelburn is the ancient home of the Earls of Glasgow and dates back to the 13th century. The **graffiti project** on the castle is a spectacular piece of artwork, surrounded by a beautiful country estate and wooded glen. There is plenty to interest all the family.

2. The island of **Great Cumbrae**, accessible via a 10-minute ferry crossing from Largs, has an undeniable charm and a fabulous setting on the Clyde with views towards Arran. The capital, Millport, is every inch the model Victorian resort, with its own museum and aquarium, as well as the Cathedral of the Isles, Europe's smallest cathedral. SportScotland National Centre Cumbrae is perfect for thrill seekers, while Country & Western fans will enjoy the week-long festival in late summer.

3. Opened in 1995, the **Isle of Arran Distillery** at Lochranza enjoys a spectacular location and is among the most recent to begin production in Scotland. The distillery has a visitor centre that offers fully guided tours, and the opportunity to pour your own bottle. Peat and artificial colourings aren't used in Arran whisky, which the distillers proudly claim offers 'the true spirit of nature'.

4. **Dean Castle** lies in Kilmarnock in East Ayrshire. Known for its astounding collection of medieval instruments and armoury, the Castle sits in a glorious country park. Dean Castle is a family favourite, with a pet corner, an adventure playground and many different woodland walks and cycle routes. Contact the Castle ahead of your visit to confirm seasonal opening hours for the Castle and its facilities.

5. For some crazy outdoor fun, head to **Loudoun Castle** in Galston – Scotland's No 1 Family Theme Park. Loudoun Castle is a terrific day out for younger kids with swashbuckling fun in the Pirates' Cove, and pony treks and tractor rides at McDougal's Farm. Open Easter – September.

6. One of the finest collections of Bronze Age **standing stones** in Scotland can be found at scenic **Machrie Moor**. Around seven separate rings of stones have been discovered on the moor, with many still undiscovered under the peat which now grows in the vicinity. Visit during the summer solstice for a truly atmospheric experience.

FOOD AND DRINK　　　　　　www.eatscotland.com

7　　With excellent **local produce** such as cheese, ale, honey, ice cream and chocolate made to the highest standard, the Ayrshire & Arran kitchen will delight the palate and ignite culinary creativity.

8　　Being on the west coast, the **seafood** is delicious and could not be fresher. Take advantage of the opportunity to visit an up-market fish and chip shop or order the seafood at one of the excellent restaurants.

9　　With such a range of natural and local ingredients to inspire, it is no wonder that Ayrshire & Arran has such fabulous **restaurants**. From Michelin Star and AA rosette winning restaurants to the best that gastro pubs have to offer, Ayrshire & Arran will satisfy the biggest gourmet's appetite.

GOLF　　　　　　www.visitscotland.com/golf

10　　Royal Troon and Turnberry Ailsa, found on the Ayrshire coastline, are two of the best **championship courses** on The Open circuit. The famous Prestwick golf course is also on the same stretch of coast. It was at Prestwick in 1860 where the first Open Championship was played. Although at that time it only attracted eight golfers, it was the beginning of competitive golf as we now know it.

11　　It is not just championship courses that Ayrshire is famous for. It is the good value and spectacular play of some of the lesser renowned courses. The charm and challenge of **hidden gems** like Belleisle, Brodick, Rountenburn, Lochgreen and Largs, to name just a few, offer brilliant golf at a very reasonable price.

12　　Scotland is not only the Home of Golf, it is the home of **links golf**, the original form of the game that had its beginnings in Scotland over 600 years ago. Ayrshire and Arran has some of the finest and most famous links golf courses in the world; Western Gailes, Glasgow Gailes, West Kilbride, Royal Troon, Prestwick, Prestwick St Nicholas, Turnberry Ailsa and Shiskine on the Isle of Arran are all part of the Great Scottish Links collection.

13　　**The Open** returns to Ayrshire in 2009. It will see the world's best professional golfers flock to the legendary links of Turnberry to take on the greatest challenge in professional golf. If previous years are anything to go by, the competition will be fierce and the sun will be shining.

WALKS

14　**The River Ayr Way** is the first source to sea path network, which follows the river from its source at Glenbuck to the sea at Ayr. Running through beautiful Ayrshire villages and countryside, the river is steeped in history and legend. With spectacular scenery and abundant wildlife it is enjoyable to walk the full 66 km / 40 mile route or just part of it.

15　Starting at Whiting Bay the 2-hour **Glenashdale Falls** walk shows off the impressive falls plummeting for about 140ft. This walk is also overflowing with history, featuring the remains of Whiting Bay Church, an Iron Age Hill Fort, and further out up a number of steps, the Giants' Graves – a group of Neolithic tombs. This easy-to-moderate walk has waymarkers and stays on footpaths and tracks.

16　As Arran's highest point, **Goatfell** is a challenging but enjoyable walk. There are two paths catering for different abilities, and those who make it to the summit may be rewarded with stunning views of Ayrshire, the Mull of Kintyre and Ireland. For the round trip from Brodick Country Park, allow around 5-6 hours.

17　**The Big Wood**, in Irvine Valley, offers a stunning one-hour walk, particularly in May when there is a virtual carpet of bluebells. Start at the A71 lay-by between Newmilns and Galston at the Hag Bridge. The walk itself gradually climbs through woodland until you reach the gate to Woodhead Farm. Tread the old Lime Road and descend gently down the 'Pit Brae' or follow the steep winding road through the Devil's Basin.

HISTORY

18　Robert Adam's fairytale **Culzean Castle**, perched on a clifftop overlooking Ailsa Craig and the Firth of Clyde, is a study in extravagance. A favourite of President Eisenhower, he was given his own apartment here by its previous owners, the Kennedys. Fans of military history should explore the Armoury, filled with antique pistols and swords. 565 acres of country park surround the Castle, with woodland walks, a walled garden and even a beach.

19　On January 25th 1759, Scotland's National Bard was born in the picturesque village of Alloway, a must for admirers of the man and his work. Here, you can visit **Burns Cottage** and a museum containing prized artefacts such as an original manuscript of Auld Lang Syne. Numerous surrounding sites, including the Brig O' Doon and Kirk Alloway, are familiar from Burns' epic poem Tam O'Shanter, which even has an entire visitor attraction dedicated to it.

20　The **Isle of Arran Heritage Museum** can be found on the main road at Rosaburn, just north of Brodick. The present group of buildings was once a working croft and smiddy, and include a farmhouse, cottage, bothy, milk house, laundry, stable, coach house and harness room. The fascinating exhibits reflect the social history, archaeology and geology of the island.

21　To visit **Dalgarven Mill**, and the Museum of Ayrshire Country Life and Costume, is to step back in time. The comprehensive exhibition of tools, machinery, horse and harness, churns, fire irons and furnishings, evokes a powerful sense of the past, which cannot fail to leave an impression. The costume collection is constantly changing, and demonstrates how fashion has evolved from 1780. The grind and splash of the wooden mill ensures the museum has an authentic ambience.

AYRSHIRE AND ARRAN

15861

Ayr

Map Ref: 1G7

Craig Tara Holiday Park
Dunure Road, Ayr, KA7 4LB
Tel:01292 265141
Web:www.touringholidays.co.uk
Jan-Dec.

Park accommodation: **875** 🚐🚙🚏🏕️🚚
Holiday caravans to let.

Leisure Facilities: 🏊🎣🎱♿

🏧🛎️♿🚻🍴Ⓡℙ🔌🍽️🎿🐾🌱🔥⛽📺☺🍽️

14938

by Girvan, Ayrshire

Map Ref: 1F8

Bennane Shore Holiday Park & Pebbles Spa

Lendalfoot, Ayrshire, KA26 0JG
Tel:01465 891233 Fax:01465 891230
Email:info@bennaneshore.com
Web:www.bennaneshore.com

The ultimate spa holiday experience awaits you with peace and tranquility on the seafront. Panoramic views to Ailsa Craig, Mull of Kintyre and Isle of Arran with brilliant sunsets. Private coastline with cliff walks, caves, cove and secluded beach. Boat slipway and fishing on-site. Luxury caravans with decks for hire with D/G and C/H - tariff from £250 - £600 p/w. Short breaks available on request. Pebbles Leisure Spa, including 15m pool, sauna, steamroom, spa, gym, restaurant and treatment rooms. Loch fishing, golf, horse riding, tennis, bowling etc. and good food can be enjoyed locally. Many places of interest to see. Highly recommended.

7 acres, Mar-Jan.

🔥🛎️🅿️🎵🔥⛽

10 Holiday Caravans to let, sleeps 1-8, £250.00-600.00 per week.

🎿🏧🍴📺☺Ⓔ🚾ℙ🛒🍽️🚲🍴

Leisure Facilities: 🏊♿🎣♿

Park accommodation: **98** 🚙🚐🚏

8 miles S of Girvan on A77 Ayr to Stranraer scenic coast road. Signposted.

Loch Ken, Dumfries & Galloway

Dumfries & Galloway

Dumfries & Galloway, like Ayrshire, also has its Burns connections as the poet spent much of his adult life in the town of Dumfries. You can even visit Ellisland Farm where he lived for many years – it's now a popular visitor attraction dedicated to his life and works.

Burns found the natural beauty of this area inspiring and you'll be equally impressed. From the Galloway Forest Park to the Solway Coast, there are so many picturesque places to see.

There's a great deal of wildlife around too. You can spot rare birds like red kites which were re-introduced to the area a few years back and around the coast, you'll see waders and wildfowl of all shapes and sizes.

Not surprisingly, such a naturally beautiful area is also a big attraction for artists. Don't forget to pay a visit to the charming town of Kirkcudbright which has a thriving artistic community and its studios and galleries are filled with fine works.

Kirkcudbright

DON'T MISS

1 **Sweetheart Abbey** is a glorious ruin, set in pretty New Abbey, with a flamboyant architectural style which sets it apart from previous Cisterian constructions. Here you'll find the origins of the word sweetheart from the fascinating love story of Devorgilla de Balliol who kept her husband's heart close to her - even beyond the grave. Devorgilla and the heart are now buried together before the high altar. Be sure to pop in to the welcoming Abbey Cottage tearoom after your visit.

2 North of Thornhill, in the shadow of the glorious Lowther Hills, is **Drumlanrig Castle**. It was built in the 17th century as a home for the first Duke of Queensberry. Surrounded by its gardens, estate and country park, there is much to explore. Look out for the resident red squirrels.

3 **Ellisland Farm**, just north of Dumfries, is where Scotland's National Bard – Robert Burns - wrote the famous song Auld Lang Syne, sung all over the world at parties and new year celebrations. It is part of the **Burns Heritage Trail** which winds its way through Ayrshire to Dumfries incorporating many of the locations that inspired his finest poetry, as well as buildings where he lived and worked.

4 Painters, artists and craftsmen have flocked to this area for centuries, no place more so than **Kirkcudbright**, now known as the Artists' Town for its historic artistic heritage. With its pastel coloured houses and traditional working harbour it is no wonder that artists flock to the town. Whether or not you have artistic flair, soak up the inspirational views on drives along the scenic country roads that criss-cross this part of the region.

5 Bookshops line the streets of **Scotland's Book Town, Wigtown**. Spend an easy day browsing and burrowing your way through the shelves before stopping in a local coffee shop for refreshment. There are around 30 book-related businesses in this small community, which hosts a book fair in May and a literary festival in early autumn. Book fans will find it difficult to leave!

6 A fabulous array of bizarre and beautiful plants flourish outdoors in Scotland's most exotic garden – **Logan Botanic Garden**. Warmed by the North Atlantic Drift, the property – under the care of the Royal Botanic Garden, Edinburgh – brings a dash of colour to the Rhinns of Galloway. The range of sub-tropical species even includes a number of palm trees, meaning you may forget where you actually are!

FOOD AND DRINK

www.eatscotland.com

7   Robert Burns' favourite 'howff' (pub) - **The Globe Inn**, Dumfries – is a continuing favourite of 'Doonhamers' (Dumfries locals) and visitors alike. Dating from 1610, the Inn has many claims to fame including being home to the ghost of Anna Park, a servant girl, and the fact that it held the first ever Burns Supper back in 1819. Burns' chair is still in the bar, but if you sit on it you must recite a line from one of his poems or buy all the customers in the bar a drink. If you ask the staff, they will show you the bedroom he used during his time as an excise man. The Globe serves breakfasts and bar lunches.

8   **Bladnoch Distillery**, by Wigtown is Scotland's most southerly distillery, dating from 1817. Learn about the traditions of making whisky and enjoy the riverside and woodland walks nearby.

9   **The Linen Room** restaurant in Dumfries has been awarded a Michelin Rising Star award, Scottish Rural Chef of the Year and Which Guide's Scottish Restaurant of the Year. Chef Russell Robertson delights with his gourmet fine dining and tasty local produce.

10 The glass encased **Gallie Craig Coffee House** is part of a unique visitor facility at the Mull of Galloway. There are spectacular panoramic views from the coffee house and terrace, built into the cliffs at the most southerly point in Scotland.

WALKS

www.visitscotland.com/walking

11 The **Southern Upland Way**, Scotland's longest waymarked walking route, runs 212 miles from the west to the east coast, traversing some beautiful hill scenery. For those who simply want a taster, start at Portpatrick, on the Rhinns of Galloway, and head up the coast to **Killantringan Lighthouse**. Watch out for the seabirds that make their home here. Alternatively, try the 8-mile section between Clatteringshaws Loch and St Johns Town of Dalry on the edge of the forest park.

12 For those seeking a slightly longer walk, head west to **Galloway Forest Park** and enjoy the astoundingly scenic circuit of Loch Trool. You could be forgiven for thinking you'd arrived in the Highlands as you enter Glen Trool, situated a few miles north of Newton Stewart, just off the Girvan road. The full circuit of the loch is around 5 miles and should take about 3 hours in good conditions.

13 The pretty mill town of **Langholm**, situated between rolling hills in the valley of the River Esk, has an entire network of scenic waymarked walks which make it an ideal base for the eager rambler. Twelve hikes of varying difficulty, most beginning from the town centre, are detailed in a leaflet available locally. The town even has its own walking festival in early June.

14 **Burns Walk** starts at the foot of Devorgilla Bridge in Dumfries and follows the River Nith on a winding and northerly path. For a short while, you head out of town and start to climb the riverbank before passing under a railway bridge and two road bridges. If you choose to stick to the riverside, you'll climb up Dalscone Bank, walking among the impressive beech trees. You'll have Burns Walk signs along the route to follow which will take you back south to the bridge where you started. Allow 1½ hours.

WILDLIFE   www.visitscotland.com/wildlife

15   Once extinct in Scotland, the graceful red kite – identifiable by its swallow-like tail – has been successfully reintroduced into many areas, not least around Loch Ken in Galloway. Here, many local businesses and accommodation providers have grouped together to form the **Galloway Red Kite Trail**, almost guaranteeing a sighting of the bird – particularly at the Bellymack Farm feeding station, where up to 30 have been seen at once!

16   The Dumfries and Galloway **Wildlife Festival** is an annual event held over two weeks in early April. See some of the region's special wildlife and get up close and personal with a countryside ranger to help you. If you have never seen a red squirrel, red kite or badger – now is your chance. Experienced wildlife watchers and beginners should both find something of interest in the festival, and look out for a range of events for the whole family.

17   **Ospreys** are back in Galloway, and in the County Buildings in Wigtown there is a room dedicated to watching wildlife where you can see live CCTV coverage of the first ospreys to have nested in Galloway for over 100 years. Nesting ospreys can now also be seen via a live video link at Caerlaverock Wetland Centre. Get an unparalleled view of ospreys sitting on their eggs and bringing up their young, the male coming back with fish to share with the female and taking over nesting duties while she eats.

18   The long coastline of the Solway Firth welcomes over 40,000 wildfowl and 83,000 waders each winter making Dumfries and Galloway an ornithologists paradise, and places such as **WWT Caerlaverock** and **Mersehead Nature Reserve** make it easy to get close to flocks of thousands of barnacle geese which travel every year from Norway to winter on the wetlands of the Solway.

ACTIVITIES

19   Dumfries and Galloway is where **cycling** all began and there's still no better place to travel on two wheels with over 400 miles of signposted cycle routes and world class mountain biking at the 7stanes centres stretching across southern Scotland. This is where the bicycle was first invented and you'll even find the only museum in Scotland devoted to the history of cycling at Drumlanrig Castle.

20   At **Galloway Sailing Centre** on Loch Ken you can really learn something new with activities on offer including sailing, windsurfing, power boating, kayaking, canoeing, archery, quad biking, mountain biking and climbing.

21   No child will want to miss visiting **Cream o' Galloway** Visitor Centre in Gatehouse of Fleet. Even if you can tear them away from the amazing variety of scrumptious ice creams, they will still be attracted to the child-friendly nature trails and adventure playground, flying fox and play barn, or you can hire a cycle for them to ride in safety.

22   Explore some of Scotland's finest scenery in the heart of Dumfries and Galloway. There are three **National Scenic Areas** – The Nith Estuary, Fleet Valley and the East Stewartry Coast – making it a great part of the world for touring.

67398

Scottish
TOURIST BOARD
★★★
HOLIDAY
PARK

Beattock, Dumfriesshire

Map Ref: 2B8

Craigielands Country Park

Craigielands Leisure Ltd, Beattock, Nr Moffat,
Dumfries and Galloway, DG10 9RE
Tel:01683 300591 / 07794 670119
Web:www.craigielandsleisure.com

56 acre parkland, open Mar-early Jan.

Park accommodation: 232

35849

Scottish
TOURIST BOARD
★★★★
HOLIDAY
PARK

Castle Douglas, Kirkcudbrightshire

Map Ref: 2A10

Loch Ken Holiday Park

Parton, Castle Douglas, Kirkcudbrightshire, DG7 3NE
Tel:01644 470282
Email:penny@lochkenholidaypark.co.uk
Web:www.lochkenholidaypark.co.uk

On the shores of Loch Ken.

Park accommodation: 85

Holiday Homes for hire, sleeps upto 6. Rates on application.

36135

Scottish
TOURIST BOARD
★★★★
TOURING
PARK

Castle Douglas, Kirkcudbrightshire

Map Ref: 2A10

Lochside Caravan & Camping Site

Lochside Park, by Carlingwark Loch, Castle Douglas,
Kirkcudbrightshire, DG7 1EZ
Tel:01556 502949 (Easter-Oct)
Tel/Fax:01556 503806 (Out of season)
Web:www.dumgal.gov.uk/lochsidecs

Site open Easter-Oct.

Park accommodation: 160

Prices from £11.00-16.00 for up to 4 persons.

21250

Scottish
TOURIST BOARD
★★★★
HOLIDAY
PARK

Thistle

Creetown, Wigtownshire

Map Ref: 1H10

Creetown Caravan Park

Silver Street, Creetown, Wigtownshire, DG8 7HU
Tel/Fax:01671 820377
Email:creetowncaravan@btconnect.com
Web:www.creetown-caravans.co.uk

3.5 acres, grassy, Mar-Oct. Extra charge for electricity,
awnings.

Park accommodation:74

22 tourers £12.00, 22 motors £12.00, 22 tents £8.00. Total Touring Pitches 22.
4 Holiday Caravans to let, sleeps 4-6, total sleeping capacity 22, £230.00-350.00 per week.

Leisure Facilities:
In village turn down between Clock Tower and Ellangowan Hotel. Down hill, left along Silver St. Signposted.

49193

Scottish
TOURIST BOARD
★★★★
HOLIDAY
PARK

Thistle

Crocketford, Dumfries

Map Ref: 2A9

Park of Brandedleys

Crocketford, Dumfries
DG2 8RG
Tel:0845 4561760 Fax:01556 690681
Email:brandedleys@holgates.com
Web:www.holgates.com

25 acres, mixed, Jan-Dec, Extra charge for awnings.

Tourers £12.50-21.00, motors £12.50-21.00, tents £12.50-21.00,
Total Touring Pitches 80.

10 Holiday Caravans to let, sleeps 4-6, total sleeping capacity 66,
£190.00-495.00 per week.

Leisure Facilities:

From Dumfries take A75 Stranraer to village of Crocketford (approx
8mls), first turning on left side of road.

Park accommodation: 160

IMPORTANT: PRICES STATED ARE ESTIMATES AND MAY BE SUBJECT TO AMENDMENTS
FOR A FULL LISTING OF QUALITY ASSURED CARAVAN AND CAMPING PARKS, PLEASE SEE DIRECTORY AT BACK OF THIS GUIDE

33

DUMFRIES AND GALLOWAY

Dumfries
Map Ref: 2B9

14338

Barnsoul Farm
Shawhead, Dumfries, DG2 9SQ
Tel:01387 730249 Fax:01387 730453
Email:barnsouldg@aol.com
Web:www.barnsoulfarm.co.uk

200 acres, mixed, Apr-Oct. Extra charge for electricity.

Park accommodation: 50
20 tourers £12.00-16.00, 20 motors £14.00-16.00, 20 tents
£10.00-14.00, Total Touring Pitches 20.
Wigwam bothies, sleeps 4-6, £25.00-30.00 per night per unit.

Leisure Facilities:
From Dumfries go 6mls towards Stranraer on A75. Turn right at signs,
Shawhead and Barnsoul. Follow signs for Barnsoul Farm. Signposted.

Gretna, Dumfriesshire
Map Ref: 2C10

58306

Braids Caravan Park
Annan Road, Gretna, DG16 5DQ
Tel:01461 337409
Email:enquiries@thebraidscaravanpark.co.uk
Web:www.thebraidscaravanpark.co.uk
6 acres, grassy, hardstanding, Jan-Dec, Extra charge
for awnings, showers.

Park accommodation: 93
84 tourers from £14.00, 60 motorhomes from £14.00, Total Touring
Pitches 90.

In Gretna on right of B721 road to Annan. Signposted.

Kippford, by Dalbeattie, Kirkcudbrightshire Map Ref: 2A10

34225

Kippford Holiday Park
Kippford, Kirkcudbrightshire, DG5 4LF
Tel:01556 620636 Fax:01556 620607
Email:info@kippfordholidaypark.co.uk
Web:www.kippfordholidaypark.co.uk

20 acres, mixed, Jan-Dec.

Park accommodation: 200
25 tourers £11.00-18.00, 25 motors £11.00-18.00, 25 tents
£11.00-18.00, Total Touring Pitches 45.
30 Holiday Caravans to let, sleeps 4-6, total sleeping capacity 150,
£120.00-505.00 per week.

Leisure Facilities:
Take A710 from Dalbeattie towards 'Colvend Coast'. In 3½ mls entrance is,
on the right off the main road. Signposted.

Kirkcudbright
Map Ref: 2A10

54708

Silvercraigs Caravan & Camping Site
Silvercraigs Road, Kirkcudbright, Kirkcudbrightshire,
DG6 4BT
Tel:01557 330123 (Easter to Oct)
Tel/Fax:01556 503806 (Out of season)
Web:www.dumgal.gov.uk/silvercraigscs

Site open Easter-Oct.

Park accommodation: 50
Prices from £11.00-16.00 for up to 4 persons.

Lochmaben, Dumfriesshire
Map Ref: 2B9

34339

Kirkloch Caravan & Camping Site
Kirk Loch Brae, Kirk Loch, Lochmaben, Dumfriesshire
Tel:07746 123783 (Easter-Oct)
Tel/Fax:01556 503806 (Out of season)
Web:www.dumgal.gov.uk/kirklochcs

Site open Easter-Oct.

Park accommodation: 30
Prices from £9.00-13.00 for up to 4 persons.

Newton Stewart, Wigtownshire
Map Ref: 1G10

65567

East Culkae Farmhouse
Sorbie, Newton Stewart, Wigtownshire, DG8 8AS
Tel:01988 850214

Park accommodation: 1
33' static, sleeps 4-6, all mod.cons. From £225.00-300.00 per week.

Scott's View, Scottish Borders

Scottish Borders

There are many lovely towns to visit in the Scottish Borders and a lot of different things to see and do. Take the four great Borders Abbeys of Dryburgh, Kelso, Jedburgh and Melrose. They were founded by King David I in the 12th century and though each is in ruins, a strong impression of their former glory remains.

Hawick is the centre of the local textile industry and you can still pick up bargain knitwear, tartans and tweeds at the many outlets and mills in the area.

Abbotsford, the former home of Sir Walter Scott, is now a visitor attraction just west of Melrose and you can also visit the writer's old courtroom in Selkirk, preserved as it was in the 1800s when he presided over trials.

There's some great walking in the Borders too with over 1,500 miles of designated walking routes.

Abbotsford House, Melrose

DON'T MISS

1 Take the B6404 St Boswells to Kelso road and turn onto the B6356, signposted to Dryburgh Abbey. About 1 mile along this road there is a junction signposting **Scott's View** to the right. Drive for about 2 miles for panoramic views of the Eildon Hills and the Borders countryside stretching out before you. A good spot for a picnic!

2 **Traquair House**, near Innerleithen, dates back to the 12th century and is said to be the oldest continuously inhabited house in Scotland. When its Bear Gates were closed in 1745, it was decreed that they should not reopen until another Stuart took the throne. Watch out for the Medieval Fayre in May and the Summer Fair in August.

3 Walk the **Berwickshire Coastal Path** from Berwick to St Abbs. The sea cliffs along this path are the highest on the east coast of Britain. Look out for the family of seals in Eyemouth harbour!

4 The four great **Borders Abbeys** of Kelso, Melrose, Jedburgh and Dryburgh are a must see for any visitor to the area. Melrose Abbey is said to be the resting place of the casket containing the heart of King Robert the Bruce. Dryburgh is the buriel place of Field Marshall Earl Haig and Sir Walter Scott. All of the abbeys are under the care of Historic Scotland. Kelso is the most incomplete and has free access. At Melrose, Jedburgh and Dryburgh an admission charge applies.

5 **Floors Castle** in Kelso is the home of the Roxburghe family. It is the largest inhabited castle in Scotland and has 365 windows, one for every day of the year. The Castle, grounds, gardens and restaurant are open from Easter to October with The Terrace Restaurant, walled gardens, playground and garden centre open all year. The Castle also hosts an extensive events calendar.

FOOD AND DRINK
www.eatscotland.com

6   At **Giacopazzi's** in Eyemouth you can enjoy award-winning fresh fish and chips and home-made ice creams. Eat in or take them out and sit on the harbourside.

7   The **Selkirk Bannock** is a combination of bread dough, butter, fruit and sugar and is a Borders classic. Try a slice with butter or indulge in a whole one available from most bakeries.

8   **Jethart Snails** and **Hawick Balls** are minty sweeties sure to satisfy even the sweetest tooth. Available widely in the Jedburgh and Hawick areas.

9   To get a real flavour of the area sample some **local cuisine**. With many bars and restaurants to choose from, the Scottish Borders draw on the regional best of the land and sea and serve it in their own individual style. There are many fine food outlets and delicatessens where local food and produce abound, and farmers' markets are held regularly in Peebles and Kelso.

WALKS
www.visitscotland.com/walking

10   The life and progress of St Cuthbert provided the inspiration for the **St Cuthbert's Way** walking route. Starting in Melrose and ending on Holy Island (Lindisfarne) it passes through rolling farmland, river valleys, sheltered woods, hills and moorland culminating in The Holy Island Causeway, passable only at low tide. The full route is 100 km / 60 miles in length but it can be broken down into shorter stages.

11   The **Borders Abbeys Way** is a circular route linking the four great ruined abbeys in Kelso, Jedburgh, Dryburgh and Melrose. The full route is 105 km / 65 miles in length and can easily be broken down into stages.

12   The **Southern Upland Way** is Britain's first official coast to coast long distance footpath. It runs from Portpatrick in the west to Cockburnspath in the east, offering superb and varied walking opportunities. Of the total route 130 km / 82 miles is in the Scottish Borders passing through or near St Mary's Loch, Traquair, Yair, Galashiels, Melrose, Lauder, Longformacus and Abbey St Bathans.

13   The **John Buchan Way** is named after the writer and diplomat who had many associations with the Scottish Borders. The 22 km / 13 mile route takes you from Peebles to Broughton and ends at the John Buchan Centre which houses a collection of photographs, books and other memorabilia.

ACTIVITIES

14   Glentress and Innerleithen in the Tweed Valley, and Newcastleton to the south have a massive reputation for some of the best **mountain biking** in the UK and beyond. Glentress is probably the best biking centre in Britain, with brilliant trails of all grades, a top-notch cafe, a bike shop with bike hire, changing and showering facilities, and a great atmosphere. Innerleithen, situated just a few miles south east of Glentress, is quite different from its better-known sister - away from the hustle and bustle, it's a venue for the more experienced rider and home to the Traquair XC black run – not for the faint-hearted! All three centres are part of the 7Stanes – seven mountain biking centres of excellence across the south of Scotland.

15   The 'Freedom of the Fairways' is Scotland's best-selling **golf** pass. It offers access to 21 superb courses ranging from the coastal course at Eyemouth to St Boswells - winner of the award for 'most friendly' 9-hole course - to the championship Roxburghe and Cardrona courses. The Freedom of the Fairways scheme runs from April to October and both senior and junior passes are available.

16   **Touring** the Scottish Borders is an absolute pleasure with many miles of quiet roads and spectacular scenery. You can travel the full width and breadth of the region easily in a day taking in stunning lochs, rivers and moorland, gentle rolling farmland, historic attractions and picturesque coastline. The Scottish Borders also hosts many rallies and 'meets' from vintage cars to scooters and caravans to the Citroën 2CV World Rally (hosted at Floors Castle in 2005).

17   The Scottish Borders has everything for the angler. From the internationally famous salmon **fishing** on the River Tweed to the excellent sea trout fishing on its tributaries; from the rainbow trout in the local lochs to the wilder brown trout in the rivers; and from the coarse fishing of the lower Tweed to the sea fishing off the Berwickshire coast; there is plenty to choose from.

WILDLIFE   **www.visitscotland.com/wildlife**

18   The elusive, native **red squirrel** can still be found in pockets throughout the Scottish Borders. Try the following places to catch a glimpse - Paxton House, nr Berwick, Tweed Valley Forest Park and the Floors Castle Estate. Anywhere with plenty of trees and peace and quiet be sure to keep your eyes peeled!

19   The **Tweed Valley Osprey Watch** has two centres; Glentress and Kailzie Gardens. Both are open from Easter until mid-August and September respectively. You can see live camera action from an osprey nest within the Tweed Valley Forest Park. Follow the progress of the family, from nest building in spring to chicks hatching in May, to fledgings in August. Both centres have a variety of interpretive materials and volunteer guides. A small admission charge applies.

20   On the Berwickshire coast, **St Abbs Head** is a National Nature Reserve and a landmark site for birdwatchers and wildlife enthusiasts. Thousands of breeding seabirds can be seen between April and August and migrating birds in October. The scenery is stunning with wide-sweeping views from the lighthouse on 'The Head' north towards Edinburgh and the Fife coast and south towards Holy Island, Bamburgh and the Farne Islands. There are a number of waymarked trails around the reserve which all start from the car park and information centre.

Neidpath Castle, Peebles

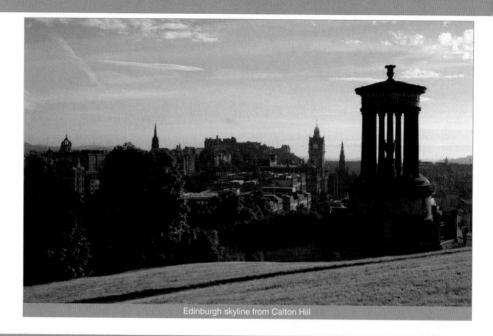

Edinburgh skyline from Calton Hill

EDINBURGH AND THE LOTHIANS

Each year, more than four million visitors arrive in Scotland's capital and discover one of the finest cities in the world.

Whether you're partying at the biggest Hogmanay celebrations on Earth or taking your seat in the audience at the planet's largest arts festival, Edinburgh always offers more than you could ever hope to take in on one visit.

Streets steeped in history

No trip to Edinburgh is complete without a visit to the world famous Castle. Over a million people take to its ramparts every year. Many then set off down the Esplanade and onto the Royal Mile touching history with every step. During the Festival weeks, hundreds of acts perform on the Mile in an explosion of colour and sound, creating an exciting mêlée that changes every day.

Although the trappings of modern life are never far away in the shops, cafés and bars, the Old Town's fascinating history is impossible to ignore. Edinburgh's ghosts whisper in the closes: grave robbers and thieves rubbing shoulders with poets, philosophers, kings and queens – each conjured up and colourfully interpreted in the museums, exhibitions and visitor attractions you'll pass along the way.

A city of beauty

The city's rich history is matched by its beauty. Architecturally, Edinburgh is a stunning city. That beauty extends to its parks, gardens and wild places – don't miss the Royal Botanic Garden, the view from the top of majestic Arthur's Seat or the Water of Leith walkway which brings a touch of the countryside right into the city.

Edinburgh is also a city by the sea with a rapidly changing seafront. The busy port of Leith has been transformed in recent years and it boasts a wonderful selection of bars and restaurants.

Get out of town

Further out of town, there's much to explore. Take a trip down the coast to places like Aberlady, Gullane, Longniddry, Dirleton, North Berwick and Dunbar. Play golf on top-class courses, watch the seabirds on beautiful sandy beaches or go on a boat trip round the Bass Rock.

You could cycle for miles along the Union Canal towpath, visit Roslin Glen and the mysterious Rosslyn Chapel, head for Linlithgow and its ruined Palace or bet on a thrilling day out at the Musselburgh races.

While most people wouldn't associate the capital city with caravans and camping, there are some fine options within Edinburgh itself as well as a splendid array of parks throughout the Lothians. So whether you fancy a seaside location or a country park, you're sure to find a superb base for a holiday in an area that will always inspire you and leave you longing for more.

Victoria Street, Edinburgh

What's On?

Dine Around Edinburgh
8 January – 4 February 2008
Excellent value fixed price meals at top Edinburgh restaurants.
www.eatscotland.com

Ceilidh Culture, Edinburgh
21 March – 13 April 2008
A vibrant celebration of traditional Scottish arts.
www.ceilidhculture.co.uk

Edinburgh International Science Festival
25 March – 5 April 2008
Quell the curiosity of inquiring minds.
www.sciencefestival.co.uk

Mary King's Ghost Fest, Edinburgh
May 2008 (dates TBC)
Explore Edinburgh's haunted places.
www.edinburghghostfest.com

Edinburgh Festival Fringe
3 – 25 August 2008
The largest arts festival on the planet.
www.edfringe.com

Edinburgh International Festival
10 – 31 August 2008
The very best of opera, theatre, music and dance.
www.eif.org.uk

Golden Oldies World Rugby Festival, Edinburgh
1 – 8 September 2008
The world's largest rugby festival for over-35s.
www.visitscotland.com/rugby

East Lothian Food & Drink Festival
September 2008 (dates TBC)
Food and entertainment for all ages.
www.foodanddrinkeastlothian.com

Edinburgh's Christmas
Late November – 24 December 2008
Edinburgh becomes a winter wonderland.
www.edinburghschristmas.com

www.edinburgh.org

All dates correct at time of publication. Please check before booking. VisitScotland cannot be held responsible for any inaccuracies.

41

DON'T MISS

1   Stroll down the **Royal Mile**, so-called due to its bookends of Edinburgh Castle at the top and the Palace of Holyroodhouse at the bottom. Browse through the wide range of quirky, independent gift shops. Upon reaching the Canongate, you will find the new Scottish Parliament building, with its striking contemporary architecture evident throughout.

2   Never a month passes without a major event or **festival** in Edinburgh, whether it be rugby in February and March, science in April, Children's Theatre in May, film in June, Jazz and Blues in July, or Christmas and Hogmanay in December. And of course, there's the world's largest international arts festival in August, taking in the Fringe, the International Festival, the Tattoo and the Book Festival. The city buzzes with excitement no matter what season you choose to come.

3   **The National Galleries of Scotland** offer a collection of some of the best Scottish and international artists in the world, housed in five galleries across Edinburgh. From Rembrandt and Monet, to Picasso and Bacon, there are also major touring exhibitions.

4   **Linlithgow Palace**, once an important royal residence and birthplace of Mary, Queen of Scots, is now a magnificent ruin. Set beside a loch, you can imagine what life must have been like in this vast palace with so many rooms, passages and stairways.

5   Within minutes of Edinburgh, you can stroll along the white sands of **East Lothian**, with only the sound of water lapping on the shore. Head for Gullane, Yellowcraig or North Berwick. The sheer expanses of beach are truly breathtaking.

6   Set amidst the beauty of Roslin Glen, the mysterious and magical **Rosslyn Chapel** is undoubtedly Scotland's most outstanding Gothic Church. According to Dan Brown's The Da Vinci Code, it is on the trail of the Holy Grail, which only adds to the intrigue.

FOOD AND DRINK

www.eatscotland.com

7 **Farmers' markets** are great ways to get the freshest quality local produce. Held every Saturday morning on Castle Terrace and the second and last Thursday of the month on Castle Street in Edinburgh, and the last Saturday of each month in Haddington in East Lothian, be sure to pop along early to pick up the very best supplies.

8 Set along the Union Canal, **The Bridge Inn**, to the west of Edinburgh, offers a great escape to the outdoors. With several child-friendly awards under its belt, it offers play areas and a children's menu.

9 For full-on romance, book ahead for a table at **The Witchery by the Castle** in Edinburgh. Its food, service and ambience consistently win awards. Located in a historic 16th century building at the gates of Edinburgh Castle, it aims to create a memorable and magical dining experience.

10 **Dine Around Edinburgh** is an initiative that allows you to experience some of Edinburgh's top restaurants at inexpensive prices. Held each January, over 25 eateries take place, from seafood to vegetarian, from the waterfront at Leith to all over the city centre.

HISTORY AND HERITAGE

11 With fantastic views over the Firth of Forth, the ship-shaped **Blackness Castle** looks almost poised to set sail, and has been used as a prison for much of its history. This was the impressive setting for Franco Zeffirelli's film of Hamlet starring Mel Gibson.

12 The **National Museum of Scotland** presents an impressive history of both our fascinating nation and that of our whole world. With a continuous programme of changing exhibitions you could happily spend the whole day here. Or why not go to the **Museum of Flight**, where you can discover the extraordinary story of our human ambition to take to the skies, and check out the Concorde Experience.

13 The **Royal Yacht** *Britannia*, former floating home of the monarchy offers a superb visitor experience that will guide you through 40 years of royal life aboard, including private family quarters, the sick bay and the laundry!

14 The ruins of 14th century **Tantallon Castle** are perched on an East Lothian cliff top, just to the south east of North Berwick. From here, look out to the Bass Rock, the largest single island gannet colony.

SHOPPING

15 In **Princes Street**, Edinburgh has one of the most beautiful shopping streets in the country with the usual high street stores along one side while on the other, in the shelter of Edinburgh Castle, Princes Street Gardens provide a nearby escape. Check out nearby **George Street** for designer stores and unique boutiques.

16 **Multrees Walk** is located in the heart of the city and is headed by Harvey Nichols. This is the prestigious street that is a must-see on a shopping trip to the city. Locally known as The Walk, shops include Emporio Armani, Louis Vuitton, Calvin Klein Underwear and Reiss.

17 Surrounding the city centre, Edinburgh has a number of urban villages where you'll find **specialist shops**, from up-and-coming designers to crafts, jewellery, food and gifts. Try Bruntsfield, Stockbridge and Leith. In the centre, try Cockburn Street, Victoria Street, and the Royal Mile for something a bit different.

ACTIVITIES AND ATTRACTIONS

18 Edinburgh and the Lothians is a superb base for **golf**, whether you choose to play some of the city's fine courses or go east to the coast. Stay in the city for the challenges of Bruntsfield Links, Prestonfield or Duddingston. Or head to the Lothians for the perfect mixture of parkland and links courses, you can enjoy inspirational views across to Fife from some courses in East Lothian.

19 There is a fantastic range of **walks** and trails throughout scenic and historic countryside around Edinburgh and the Lothians. Through the heart of the city runs the Water of Leith where a peaceful path offers a handy escape from the vibrant centre. In East Lothian the stretch of beach from Gullane to Yellowcraig is perfect for a walk or a picnic. Or climb Arthur's Seat for a phenomenal view of the Scottish Lowlands.

20 The area is home to some of Scotland's most impressive visitor **attractions**. From interactive exhibits to wonders of the natural world, there is something for everyone. Head to the Scottish Seabird Centre in North Berwick or Edinburgh Zoo to see wildlife up close, travel back in time at Our Dynamic Earth, try rock climbing at Edinburgh International Climbing Arena or venture underground at The Real Mary King's Close.

21 With free entry to over 30 top attractions, free return airport and city centre bus transport, a free comprehensive guidebook as well as loads of exclusive offers, the **Edinburgh Pass** is the best way to discover all that Edinburgh has to offer. Buy a 1, 2 or 3 day Pass from www.edinburghpass.com or from one of the Tourist Information Centres in Edinburgh.

MAP

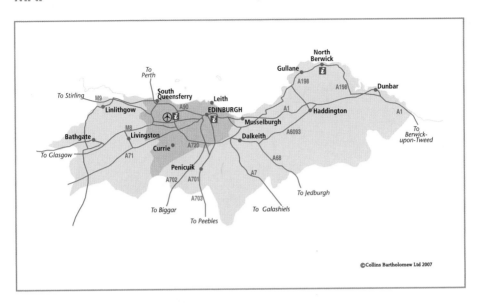

©Collins Bartholomew Ltd 2007

TOURIST INFORMATION CENTRES

Edinburgh & Lothians	
Edinburgh Airport	Main Concourse, Edinburgh International Airport, Edinburgh EH12 9DN
Edinburgh & Scotland Information Centre	Princes Mall, 3 Princes Street, Edinburgh EH2 2QP
North Berwick	1 Quality Street, North Berwick EH39 4HJ

Make the most of your stay in Scotland and make your first stop the Tourist Information Centre wherever you go.

Knowledgeable and friendly staff can help you with information and advice; they can answer your questions, book accommodation and you can even pick up some souvenirs to take home for friends and family.

For information and ideas about exploring Scotland in advance of your trip, call our booking and information service or go to **www.visitscotland.com**

Call **0845 22 55 121**

or if calling from outside the UK call **+44 (0) 1506 832 121**

From Ireland call **1800 932 510**

A £4 booking fee applies to telephone bookings of accommodation.

67622

Dunbar, East Lothian
Map Ref: 2E4

Belhaven Bay Caravan & Camping Park

Belhaven Bay, Edinburgh Road, Dunbar, East Lothian
EH42 1TU
Tel:01368 865956 Fax:01368 865022
Email:belhaven@meadowhead.co.uk
Web:www.meadowhead.co.uk

20 acres, mixed, Extra charge for awnings.

Park accommodation: 112

42 tourers £12.00-21.00, motorhomes £12.00-21.00, 10 tents
£12.00-19.50 per night. Total Touring Pitches 52.

7 Holiday Caravans to let, sleeps 6-8, total sleeping capacity 50,
£65.00-130.00 per night.

Leisure Facilities:
From A1 North or South exit at Thistly Cross r/about & follow signs to Dunbar and
Bellhaven Bay which is on left-hand side after about a miles drive.

63596

East Calder, West Lothian
Map Ref: 2B5

Linwater Caravan Park

West Clifton, East Calder, EH53 0HT
Tel:0131 333 3326 Fax:0131 333 1952
Email:linwater@supanet.com
Web:www.linwater.co.uk

4 acres, grassy, level, hardstanding, mid Mar-Oct.

50 tourers £12.00-15.00, 50 motors £12.00-15.00,, 10 tents
£10.00-13.00, Total Touring Pitches 60.

Leisure Facilities: We are situated on a minor road off B7030 which
runs between Wilkieston on, A71 and J1, Newbridge on M9.
Signposted.

Park accommodation: 60

39087

Edinburgh
Map Ref: 2C5

Mortonhall Caravan & Camping Park

Frogston Road, Edinburgh, EH16 6TJ
Tel:0131 664 1533 Fax:0131 664 5387
Email:mortonhall@meadowhead.co.uk
Web:www.meadowhead.co.uk

26 acres, mixed. Extra charge for awnings.

Park accommodation: 268

250 tourers £12.25-26.00, 250 motors £12.25-26.00, 250 tents £11.25-22.00, Total Touring Pitches 250.
19 Holiday Caravans to let, sleeps 6-8, total sleeping capacity 139, £255.00-760.00 per week, Wigwams
£13.00-19.00 per night (Min 2 sharing).

Leisure Facilities:
From North or South follow signs from A720 City by-pass onto A701 or A702, from which Mortonhall is
signed. From City Centre leave heading South on either A701 or A702 following signs for Mortonhall at
the B701 junction south of the City by-pass. Alternatively from Princes Street (garden side). Lothian bus
11 with destination Kaimes or the other side take bus 31 (shop side) destination Fairmilehead.

14668

Linlithgow, West Lothian
Map Ref: 2B4

Beecraigs Caravan and Camping Site

Beecraigs Country Park, Linlithgow, West Lothian
EH49 6PL
Tel:01506 844516 Fax:01506 846256
Email:mail@beecraigs.com
Web:www.beecraigs.com

Jan-Dec.

Take J3 or 4 off M9 Mway to Linlithgow. Follow signs for Beecraigs
Country Park - 2 mls up Preston Road. Turn left at top of Hill Road
and then 1st right. Signposted.

Park accommodation: 39

| 54223 | Longniddry, East Lothian | Map Ref: 2D4 |

Seton Sands Holiday Village
Longniddry, East Lothian, EH32 0QF
Tel:01875 813333 Fax:01875 813531
Email:lee.mckay@bourne-leisure.co.uk
Web:www.setonsands-park.co.uk

14 Mar-31 Oct

Park accommodation: 630
10 tents from £9.00-44.00, 28 electric pitches from £12.00-60.00.
210 Holiday caravans to let, from £119.00-689.00.
Leisure Facilities:

| 23304 | Musselburgh, East Lothian | Map Ref: 2C5 |

Drummohr Caravan Park
Levenhall, Musselburgh, Edinburgh, EH21 8JS
Tel:0131 665 6867 Fax:0131 653 6859
Email:bookings@drummohr.org
Web:www.drummohr.org

10 acres, mixed, Mar-Oct. Extra charge for awnings,
showers.

Park accommodation: 108
80 tourers £13.00-16.00, 80 motors £13.00-16.00, tents £13.00-16.00.
Total Touring Pitches 108.
Leisure Facilities:
From A1 follow caravan park signs situated between the B1361 and
B1348. Signposted.

| 36446 | Newtongrange, Midlothian | Map Ref: 2C5 |

Lothian Bridge Caravan Park
Newtongrange, Dalkeith, EH22 4TP
Tel:0131 663 6120 Fax:0131 663 6266
Email:lothianbridge@tiscali.co.uk

4 acres, grassy, level, hardstanding, Apr-6 Jan. Extra
charge for electricity, awnings. Small dogs only by
permission.

Park accommodation: 50
46 tourers £12.00-16.00, 46 motors £12.00-16.00, 30 tents £10.00. Total
Touring Pitches 46.
7 mls S of Edinburgh on A7 Galashiels-Edinburgh. 1 ml from Mining
Museum. Signposted.

| 37916 | North Berwick, East Lothian | Map Ref: 2D4 |

Tantallon Caravan & Camping Park
Dunbar Road, North Berwick, East Lothian, EH39 5NJ
Tel:01620 893348 Fax:01620 895623
Email:tantallon@meadowhead.co.uk
Web:www.meadowhead.co.uk

18 acres, grassy, sloping, hardstanding, Mar-Oct. Extra
charge for awnings.

Park accommodation: 207
147 tourers £16.00-22.00, 147 motors £16.00-22.00, 70 tents £12.00-20.00. Total Touring
Pitches 147.
10 Holiday Caravans to let, sleeps 6, total sleeping capacity 70, caravan holiday homes
£45.00-95.00 per night, wigwams £35.00-50.00 per night.
Leisure Facilities:
From North turn off A1 at Abbotsview Junction (Haddington) follow A199 for 7mls then turn
left on A198 and follow signs for North Berwick. We are on right after 6½ miles. From A1
South exit at Thistly Cross r/bout and follow signs to North Berwick and Tantallon Park is on
right-hand side before North Berwick.

IMPORTANT: PRICES STATED ARE ESTIMATES AND MAY BE SUBJECT TO AMENDMENTS
FOR A FULL LISTING OF QUALITY ASSURED CARAVAN AND CAMPING PARKS, PLEASE SEE DIRECTORY AT BACK OF THIS GUIDE

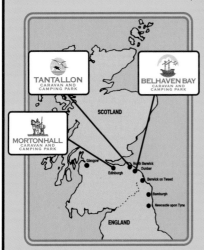

Princes Street from Calton Hill, Edinburgh

George Square, Glasgow

GREATER GLASGOW AND CLYDE VALLEY

Glasgow is a must-visit city. Stylish, flamboyant, confident and imaginative, Glasgow buzzes from early morning until late at night.

There's so much choice it's difficult to know where to start and even harder to know when to stop. And wherever you go in Scotland's largest city, you'll be overwhelmed by the irresistible friendliness of its inhabitants.

Shop 'til you drop

It's easy to get caught up in Glasgow's fast-moving social whirl – especially if you like shopping. Outside of London, there isn't a UK city that can touch Glasgow for quantity and quality.

If you're in need of retail therapy you'll revel in the elegance of Princes Square, the diversity of the Buchanan Galleries and the classy opulence of the Italian Centre in the chic Merchant City.

Glasgow is easily Scotland's most fashion-conscious city and its passion for all things stylish brings an exciting edge to its boutiques and malls.

That passion spills over into the cafés and bars, the boutique hotels, the restaurants, nightclubs, theatres and music venues. Glasgow nightlife is always exhilarating whether you're checking out the next hit band at King Tut's, watching ground-breaking theatre at Oran Mor or just sipping a pint in Ashton Lane.

Haute cuisine

Foodies love Glasgow too. From traditional afternoon tea at One Devonshire Gardens or the Willow Tearooms to every major culinary style in the world, Glasgow's restaurants have a rapidly growing international reputation.

Art for art's sake

Glasgow is an art lover's delight too. The impressive legacy of its most eminent architectural sons, Charles Rennie Mackintosh and Alexander 'Greek' Thomson can be seen in the city's streets and its galleries and museums host one of Europe's biggest collections of civic art. Don't miss Kelvingrove Art Gallery and Museum (recently restored at a cost of £27.9 million) or the Burrell Collection in Pollock Country Park.

Despite the endless hustle and bustle, peace and tranquillity are never far away. Glasgow is known as the 'dear green place' and there are over 70 parks and gardens in the city where you can escape for a while.

Beyond the city limits, you can trace the river back through the Clyde Valley all the way to the picturesque Falls of Clyde in Lanarkshire, just beside the immaculately preserved village of New Lanark which is a World Heritage site.

On the Clyde coast you can take a trip 'doon the watter' in the P.S. Waverley, the world's last sea-going paddle steamer. At Strathclyde Country Park near Hamilton and Mugdock Country Park near Milngavie you'll enjoy a wide range of outdoor activities including walking, cycling, horse riding, sailing, canoeing and much more.

Glasgow's maritime history can be explored at Braehead and Paisley is just a short journey away. Don't miss the impressive Paisley Abbey which dates back to 1163.

Although the city of Glasgow isn't an obvious location for caravans and campers, there are some excellent facilities nearby. Strathclyde Country Park near Motherwell has a touring park and there are others within easy reach both in the Clyde Valley and further afield. Once you've established a base, it's easy to get into Glasgow and you'll be glad you made the visit.

Kelvingrove Art Gallery and Museum, Glasgow

What's On?

Celtic Connections, Glasgow
16 January – 3 February 2008
Three weeks of the best in Celtic music from around the globe.
www.celticconnections.com

Magners Glasgow International Comedy Festival
6 - 23 March 2008
The largest comedy festival in the UK.
www.glasgowcomedyfestival.com

Paisley Beer Festival
28 April – 3 May 2008
Scotland's largest real ale festival, with well over 100 real ales on tap.
www.paisleybeerfestival.org.uk

West End Festival, Glasgow
13 – 29 June 2008
Arts festival celebrating the city's bohemian West End.
www.westendfestival.co.uk

World Pipe Band Championships and Piping Live: Glasgow International Piping Festival
11-17 August 2008
A week of piping events across Glasgow.
www.pipingfestival.co.uk

Gourmet Glasgow
August 2008 (dates TBC)
A month-long festival of food and drink.
www.gourmetglasgow.com

Kirkintilloch Canal Festival
August 2008 (dates TBC)
Two days of fun in the 'Canal Capital of Scotland'.
www.kirkintillochcanalfestival.org.uk

Classic Car Rally, Chatelherault Country Park
August 2008 (dates TBC)
Vintage and classic cars on display.
www.visitlanarkshire.com

Merchant City Festival, Glasgow
September 2008 (dates TBC)
Festival celebrating the cultural richness of the city's old commercial quarter.
www.merchantcityfestival.com

Glasgow's Hogmanay
31 December 2008 – 1 January 2009
Top bands, traditional music, DJs, and special guests.
www.winterfestglasgow.com

www.seeglasgow.com

DON'T MISS

1   **Kelvingrove Art Gallery and Museum** - Scotland's most visited museum - re-opened in 2006 following a three-year, £27.9 million restoration. It now has over 8,000 objects on display over three floors – 4,000 more than ever before. Old favourites and exciting new arrivals are waiting to welcome you. Forget everything you think you know about museums – Kelvingrove is different.

2   Step back in time at the 5-star, award-winning **New Lanark World Heritage Site**. The beautifully restored 18th century cotton mill village has a wonderful sense of space with plenty to keep the whole family amused. The ghost of mill-girl Annie McLeod tells you about her life in the village, then you can ride into the future in the new Millenium Experience to see how Harmony lives in the 23rd century. From here explore the Falls of Clyde Visitor Centre and Wildlife Reserve.

3   It's all about fun when you're on your holidays but what if at the same time, you could sneak in a bit of learning? **Glasgow Science Centre** has the answer. Easily accessible from Glasgow city centre by car, subway, train or bus, the Centre stands tall and instantly recognisable on the River Clyde. The interactive exhibits can keep not only the children entertained but the adults too and that's before you hit the IMAX cinema and the Scottish Power Planetarium.

4   Experience Glasgow's celebrated maritime history at **The Tall Ship**. A sight to behold, you can tour this beautiful vessel – the SV Glenlee – and discover life during its sea-faring days. Exhibitions on board tell the incredible story of its crew during four circumnavigations of the globe. On the quayside and in the Pumphouse Visitor Centre, discover more about the history of the Clyde and the Glasgow Harbour area.

5   Scotland's Centre for Architecture, Design and the City is suitably situated in the old Glasgow Herald Newspaper building which was design by Charles Rennie Mackintosh. Spanning six floors, **The Lighthouse** provides an unrivalled opportunity to experience architecture and design through a changing programme of exhibitions. The Lighthouse also contains the award winning Mackintosh Centre and Mackintosh Tower which offers stunning views of the city.

6   Charles Rennie Mackintosh designed the **Glasgow School of Art** in 1896. Today, over 100 years later, the Glasgow School of Art is still a working art school attracting talented students from all over the world. A tour will take you along the corridors of the School, through the Mackintosh Gallery and Furniture Gallery to finish in one of Mackintosh's most celebrated interiors, the Library. Along the way you will learn about Mackintosh's life and the history of the Glasgow School of Art.

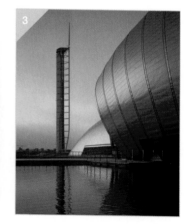

FOOD AND DRINK

www.eatscotland.com

7   **Arisaig Restaurant** is a smartly presented restaurant and bar which offers some of the best Scottish cuisine. The menu is divided into "The Land" and "The Sea" with choices of the freshest of Scottish ingredients including haggis, Stornoway black pudding, Shetland monkfish, South Uist smoked salmon and Buccleuch beef, as well as long forgotten ingredients such as kale and cairgein. The food is served in a relaxed atmosphere with friendly service.

8   With a motto like "Think Global Eat Local" it is not surprising that the menu at **Stravaigin** has been built from diverse world influences while focusing on the best of Scottish ingredients. The result is a collection of eclectic and globe trotting dishes. Stravaigin is an excellent example of West End dining.

9   **Michael Caine at ABode Glasgow** is situated in the recently opened boutique hotel ABode, which itself is in an historic Edwardian building. The restaurant has recently received an EatScotland Gold Award which recognises outstanding standards in quality and service. This truly is an excellent dining experience with the modern menu utilising the best of Scotland's seasonal larder.

10 **Uplawmoor Hotel & Restaurant** is a relaxed and friendly establishment with professional and attentive service. Originally an old beamed barn, it has been tastefully converted and offers a cosy atmosphere and a choice of imaginative à la carte or seasonal table d'hote menus.

ACTIVITIES

11 Ten miles north of Glasgow is the 750-acre **Mugdock Country Park**. Embracing unspoiled countryside at the foot of the Campsie Fells, Mugdock offers a gentle introduction to hardy walkers starting out on the 96-mile West Highland Way. The less energetic can stay a while and enjoy horse riding, archery and orienteering, among other activities.

12 At **Strathclyde Country Park** you'll find 1,000 acres of mature woodlands, wetlands, wildlife refuges and open parkland surrounding Strathclyde Loch, with a variety of activities to try out from pedalos to water skiing, orienteering to mountain biking. A good starting point for exploring is the visitor centre. Keep an eye out for otters, roe deer and the other 150 species living in the park, which is also home to Scotland's first theme park, M & D's.

13 As you enter through the main doors of **Xscape** you can watch brave souls hanging from the ceiling as they have a go on the state of the art aerial adventure course. The Centre houses numerous outdoor shops, restaurants, bars, bowling, rock climbing and much more. However, without a doubt the piece-de-résistance is the incredible SnoZone which allows you to experience indoor skiing, snowboarding or sledging on the UK's biggest real snow slope.

14 Charles Rennie Mackintosh is considered the father of the 'Glasgow Style', with his motifs instantly recognisable to visitors. He was a true visionary who worked almost exclusively in the city. His legacy lives on and can be enjoyed with the help of a **Mackintosh Trail** ticket giving admission to all associated attractions in and around Glasgow including the School of Art, Scotland Street School House, House for an Art Lover and the Mackintosh Church.

SHOPPING

15 Buchanan Street is arguably one of the classiest major shopping thoroughfares in Britain. With a tempting mix of big high street names, alternative retailers and designer outlets, it's deservedly popular. Buchanan Galleries at the top of the street offers even more shopping opportunities.

16 Situated on Buchanan Street in the heart of Glasgow's shopping district, Princes Square is home to many of the world's best known lifestyle brands. A truly exquisite venue, Princes Square presents a sophisticated alternative to Scotland's high street and a stylish destination for both dining and drinking.

17 Visitors in search of the city's chic and modern side should head to the Merchant City. Beautiful Victorian buildings, many of them former tobacco warehouses, are now the place to be seen at weekends. Trawl through innovative boutiques in search of that must-have item.

18 With strong Italian heritage, it's only fitting that there should be somewhere to purchase the latest fashions from Milan. The Italian Centre may be easier on the eye than on the pocket, but it's ideal for a treat.

19 Glasgow is often complimented for its European flavour, and nowhere is this more in evidence than on Byres Road, with its fruit and veg stalls, butchers and fishmongers flanking hip record stores and clothing retailers. Head to the West End for some wonderful eateries in the mews lanes off Byres Road.

HERITAGE AND CULTURE

20 Take in a football match for 90 minutes you'll never forget. It would be an understatement to say that Glaswegians have a passion for the beautiful game, and Glasgow is the only city in the UK to support three 50,000+ capacity football stadiums. Situated within the national stadium, Hampden the Scottish Football Museum is an essential attraction for all football fans.

21 From Celtic Connections each January to the Miller Glasgow International Comedy Festival in March and Piping Live! in August, no matter when you arrive in Glasgow and Clyde Valley you'll find live performances, events and festivals and entertainment.

22 Situated within beautiful Bellahouston Park, the House for an Art Lover was inspired by Charles Rennie Mackintosh designs from 1901. The Art Lovers' Cafe and Shop house changing art exhibitions and visitors are entertained throughout the year with a programme of dinner concerts and afternoon music recitals.

23 Chatelherault Country Park hosts the magnificently restored hunting lodge and summer house built in 1732 by William Adam for the Duke of Hamilton. The 500-acre country park, set amongst ancient oaks along the Avon Water, boasts extensive woodland walks and a visitor centre with exhibitions on the area's history, wildlife, and also the story of Chatelherault itself.

MAP

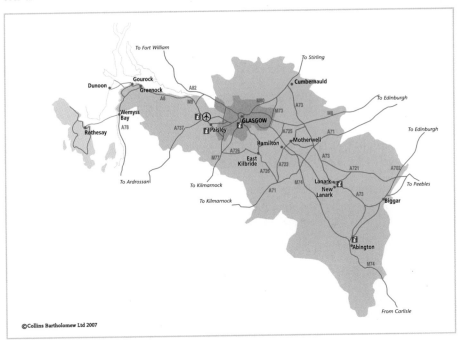

©Collins Bartholomew Ltd 2007

TOURIST INFORMATION CENTRES

Greater Glasgow & Clyde Valley

Abington	Welcome Break, Motorway Service Area, Junction 13, M74 Abington ML12 6RG
Glasgow	11 George Square, Glasgow G2 1DY
Glasgow Airport	International Arrivals Hall, Glasgow International Airport, PA3 2ST
Lanark	Horsemarket, Ladyacre Road, Lanark ML11 7QL
Paisley	9A Gilmour Street, Paisley PA1 1DD

Make the most of your stay in Scotland and make your first stop the Tourist Information Centre wherever you go.

Knowledgeable and friendly staff can help you with information and advice; they can answer your questions, book accommodation and you can even pick up some souvenirs to take home for friends and family.

For information and ideas about exploring Scotland in advance of your trip, call our booking and information service or go to www.visitscotland.com

Call 0845 22 55 121

or if calling from outside the UK call +44 (0) 1506 832 121

From Ireland call 1800 932 510

A £4 booking fee applies to telephone bookings of accommodation.

20918

Craigendmuir Park

Craigendmuir Park Business Centre, Stepps, Glasgow,
7G33 6AF
Tel:0141 779 2973   Fax:0141 779 4057
Email:info@craigendmuir.co.uk
Web:www.craigendmuir.co.uk

Touring caravan and camping area available. Rates on application.

Chalet and Holiday Homes for hire, sleeps upto 6. Rates on application.

Park accommodation: 101

Shopping in Glasgow

Kelvingrove Art Gallery and Museum, Glasgow

IMPORTANT: PRICES STATED ARE ESTIMATES AND MAY BE SUBJECT TO AMENDMENTS
FOR A FULL LISTING OF QUALITY ASSURED CARAVAN AND CAMPING PARKS, PLEASE SEE DIRECTORY AT BACK OF THIS GUIDE

57

Oban, Argyll

WEST HIGHLANDS AND ISLANDS, LOCH LOMOND, STIRLING AND TROSSACHS

Contrast is the word that best sums up an area that spans Scotland from the shores of the Forth in the east to the very tip of Tiree in the west. Here the Highlands meet the Lowlands and geography and cultures diverge.

For the visitor, the endlessly changing landscape means a rich and varied holiday experience.

There are rugged high mountains, spectacular freshwater lochs, fascinating islands and dramatic seascapes. You'll find pretty villages, mill towns and Scotland's newest city.

And you can discover the birthplace of the Scots nation and visit places that witnessed some of the most dramatic scenes in Scotland's history.

So where do you begin? In the east, the flat plain of the Forth Valley stretches up from the River Forth towards the little towns of the Hillfoots and the Ochil Hills behind.

You can visit Scotland's smallest county – Clackmannanshire, or the 'Wee County' as it is known. And while you're in the area, head for Dollar Glen and the magnificent Castle Campbell, once the Lowland stronghold of the Clan Campbell.

Moving to the Hillfoot towns you'll be tracing the roots of Scotland's textile industry which has thrived here for many years. Visit the Mill Trail Visitor Centre in Alva to learn the history of the local woollen industry.

New city, ancient history

Beyond Alva to the west lies Stirling – one of the most important places in Scottish history thanks to its strategically important location at the gateway to the Highlands.

Once, whoever controlled Stirling, controlled Scotland. Its impressive castle stands guard over all it surveys and was the capital for the Stewart Kings. No fewer than seven battle sites can be seen from the Castle ramparts – including Stirling Bridge, a scene of triumph for William Wallace and Bannockburn where Robert the Bruce led the Scots to victory in 1314.

A National Park on your doorstep

From Stirling, it is easy to take advantage of the natural treasures of Loch Lomond and The Trossachs National Park. And that means 20 Munros (mountains over 3,000ft) to climb, 50 rivers to fish, 22 lochs to sail and thousands of miles of road and track to cycle. And when you've had your fill of activities, head for Loch Lomond Shores for a wonderful cultural and retail experience.

A place in history

Further west still, the West Highlands and Islands are waiting to be explored. Follow the whisky trail round Islay an Jura. Or jump on a ferry at Gourock and explore The Cowal Peninsula with its sea lochs and deep forests.

You could also head for lovely Lochgilphead and beyond to Kilmartin where you can trace the very roots of the nation where the Scots arrived from Ireland in the 6th century.

Choosing a holiday destination in an area as diverse as this will always be difficult but the stunning array of caravan and camping accommodation options will help. There are some wonderful holiday parks with splendid facilities in superb, unspoilt locations so you'll easily find somewhere to enjoy a perfect holiday.

Port Ellen Distillery, Isle of Islay

What's On?

Lomond and Clyde Springfest, Helensburgh
26 April – 2 May 2008
A springtime festival with a touch of Japanese culture.
www.lomondclydespringfest.co.uk

Highlands and Islands Music and Dance Festival, Oban
1 – 4 May 2008
New events and competition classes every year, 2008 is the 25th anniversary.
www.obanfestival.org

Isle of Bute Jazz Festival
1 – 5 May 2008
A host of well-known names in Bute's annual jazz-fest.
www.butejazz.com

Big in Falkirk
3 – 4 May 2008
Scotland's National Street Arts Festival.
www.biginfalkirk.com

Stirling Highland Games
13 July 2008
A great Scottish day out for the whole family.
www.stirling-highland-games.co.uk

Loch Lomond Food and Drink Festival
September (dates TBC)
Enjoy fine food and drink from all over the region.
www.lochlomondfood anddrinkfestival.com

Cowalfest
3 – 12 October 2008
Scotland's largest combined walking and arts festival.
www.cowalfest.org

Tunnocks Tour of Mull Rally
10 – 12 October 2008
Enjoy the atmosphere at this annual car rally.
www.2300club.org

Aberfoyle Mushroom Festival
16 – 19 October 2008
A long weekend of fantasy, fungi, food and fun.
www.visitaberfoyle.com

www.visitscottishheartlands.com

All dates correct at time of publication. Please check before booking. VisitScotland cannot be held responsible for any inaccuracies.

59

MAP

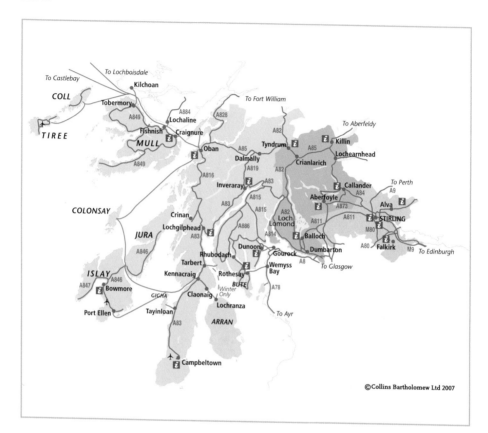

©Collins Bartholomew Ltd 2007

TOURIST INFORMATION CENTRES

West Highlands

Bowmore	The Square, Bowmore, Isle of Islay PA43 7JP
Campbeltown	Mackinnon House, The Pier, Campbeltown PA28 6EF
Craignure	The Pier, Craignure, Isle of Mull PA65 6AY
Dunoon	7 Alexandra Parade, Dunoon, PA23 8AB
Inveraray	Front Street, Inveraray PA32 8UY
Lochgilphead	Lochnell Street, Lochgilphead PA31 8JL
Oban	Argyll Square, Oban PA34 4AR
Rothesay	Winter Gardens, Rothesay, Isle of Bute PA20 0AJ

Loch Lomond

Aberfoyle	Trossachs Discovery Centre, Main Street, Aberfoyle FK8 3UQ
Callander	Rob Roy Centre, Ancaster Square, Callander FK17 8ED
Killin	Breadalbane Folklore Centre, Main Street, Killin FK21 8XE
Loch Lomond	National Park Gateway Centre, Loch Lomond Shores, Balloch G83 8QL
Tyndrum	Main Street, Tyndrum FK20 8RY

Stirling & Trossachs

Alva	Mill Trail Visitor Centre, Alva FK12 5EN
Falkirk	2-4 Glebe Street, Falkirk FK1 1HU
Stirling (Dumbarton Rd)	41 Dumbarton Road, Stirling FK8 2LQ
Stirling (Pirnhall)	Motorway Service Area, Junction 9, M9

Make the most of your stay in Scotland and make your first stop the Tourist Information Centre wherever you go.

Knowledgeable and friendly staff can help you with information and advice; they can answer your questions, book accommodation and you can even pick up some souvenirs to take home for friends and family.

For information and ideas about exploring Scotland in advance of your trip, call our booking and information service or go to www.visitscotland.com

Call 0845 22 55 121

or if calling from outside the UK call +44 (0) 1506 832 121

From Ireland call 1800 932 510

A £4 booking fee applies to telephone bookings of accommodation.

Tobermory, Isle of Mull

West Highlands and Islands

Take a journey around some of Scotland's most magical isles and penisulas and savour the atmosphere of the rugged west coast. The attraction of island life is a powerful draw for visitors, and while there are parts of the mainland around Kintyre which feel more like island than mainland, if you're looking for the genuine island experience, you'll be spoiled for choice.

There are many islands to explore including Gigha, Jura, Islay and Colonsay. And no trip to these parts would be complete without visiting Oban, the gateway to the isles, from where boats make their way to and from the likes of Mull, Coll, Tiree and Iona.

Highlights are Islay for the whisky, Iona which is deeply spiritual, and Mull, where you can see colourful Tobermory (or Balamory as families with young children will recognise it). On your way to the isles stop off in Oban, its harbour is always bustling and the area around the port has a great selection of shops, bars and restaurants.

Isle of Jura, Inner Hebrides

DON'T MISS

1. Wherever you travel in this area, you're never far from a whisky distillery. Islay alone is home to eight working distilleries, producing world-famous whiskies such as Laphroaig and Bowmore, renowned for their peaty qualities. Here, you'll also find Kilchoman, a recently opened farm distillery. The neighbouring Isle of Jura manufactures its own popular malt, while Campbeltown on Kintyre now boasts two local whiskies, Springbank and Glengyle, the latter dating from only 2004. Facilities and opening hours vary.

2. Iona is a beautiful island with white beaches and turquoise sea. Situated off the western tip of the Ross of Mull, it is one of the world's foremost centres of Christian pilgrimage. Staffa is Iona's northerly neighbour where basalt lava has created some of Europe's most astonishing rock formations which are at their most impressive at Fingal's Cave.

3. Any trip which takes in the breathtaking Argyll coastline or Argyll's Atlantic Islands, known as Scotland's Sea Kingdom, promises a memorable experience. Negotiate the Gulf of Corryvreckan with its famous whirlpool and travel round Scarba while looking out for whales, dolphins, deer and eagles, or venture further to the remote Garvellachs. You can sail from Ardfern with Craignish Cruises, from Craobh Haven with Farsain Cruises or from Easdale with Seafari Adventures or Sealife Adventures.

4. Mount Stuart on the Isle of Bute was the ancestral home of the Marquess of Bute. Today it is a high quality, award-winning attraction featuring magnificent Victorian Gothic architecture and design together with contemporary craftsmanship. Mount Stuart is surrounded by 300 acres of gloriously maintained grounds and gardens.

5. Kilmartin Glen is home to a myriad of Neolithic and Bronze Age monuments, coupled with early Christian carved stones and ruined castles. South of Oban, this site was capital of the ancient Celtic kingdom of Dalriada, as evidenced at Dunadd Fort, where a footprint in the stone is thought to have featured in royal inauguration ceremonies.

6. The common characteristic of the Glorious Gardens of Argyll & Bute is their individuality. Each garden has a variety of terrain; many are mainly level with smooth paths, while some are steep and rocky. The Gardens range from informal woodland gardens to beautiful classic examples of 18th century design.

FOOD AND DRINK
www.eatscotland.com

7   The original Loch Fyne Oyster Bar and shop started in a small shed in the lay-by at the head of Loch Fyne in the early 1980s. In 1985 it moved into the old cow byre at Clachan Farm. It has been listed in the Good Food Guide every year since then.

8   At Chatters Restaurant in Dunoon the very best of Scottish produce is prepared and served in unique surroundings. If the weather is nice a meal can be enjoyed in the lovely garden and there are regular art exhibitions to enjoy. Chatters also has a great selection of wines and a heavenly pudding trolley.

9   The Seafood Trail takes you through some of the most spectacular coastal scenery Scotland has to offer, and enables seafood lovers to sample, share and enjoy seafood and shellfish from a wide variety of waterfront establishments.

10   For centuries the west coast of Scotland and whisky have been synonymous. The so-called Whisky Coast blends incredible Scottish scenery with the best single malt whisky for a truly unforgettable experience. Getting to and around the Whisky Coast is surprisingly easy for the independent traveller in search of stunning landscapes and the finest whiskies, as the area is well served by road, rail, air and ferry.

WILDLIFE
www.visitscotland.com/wildlife

11   There are numerous operators that offer sea trip safaris around the Oban and Mull area where you can spot majestic wildlife against a backdrop of spectacular scenery. The wildlife in this area is magnificent and you may well see the majestic sea eagle, golden eagle, or a range of seabirds along with seals, dolphins, porpoise and the occasional minke whale.

12   The extensive Argyll Forest Park offers a perfect introduction to Loch Lomond & The Trossachs National Park. Start at the Ardgartan Visitor Centre on the A83 at the north of Loch Long, where the Boathouse and Riverside walks provide options for pushchairs. You'll also find cycle paths, a play area and refreshments. With its spectacular mountains, glens, lochs and woodlands, many claim that Britain's first forest park is also the finest.

13   The islands of Islay and Jura are something of a mecca for wildlife lovers. With well over a hundred breeding bird species in summer, and some of Europe's largest populations of wintering wildfowl, they are a year round destination for ornithologists. Add to this some exceptional marine wildlife, including minke whales, common and bottlenose dolphins, basking sharks and literally thousands of seals, alongside some of Britain's best opportunities to spy otters, red deer and golden eagles, and you have a natural paradise. A particular highlight is the arrival of around 50,000 barnacle and white-fronted geese from the Arctic Circle each autumn.

14   Wildlife and Bird Watching safaris offer the chance to explore the remote areas of Mull with experienced guides to help you spot and learn about the wildlife which inhabits the island. This is your chance to see golden eagles, otters, harriers and merlin to name a few.

WALKS

www.visitscotland.com/walking

15 Lismore is a lovely location to get away from it all and is easy to reach by boat from Oban. The island is just 12 miles long and 1.5 miles at its widest point, and offers many interesting walks with spectacular views of the sea and mountains. Kerrera is a beautiful island where it is also possible to walk round the entire island although this walk is about 10 miles and will take some time.

16 The wonderfully unexplored Kintyre Peninsula boasts hidden coves, deserted beaches, tiny fishing communities, gentle hills, fabulous local produce and welcoming friendly people. Stretching from Tarbert to Southend, the waymarked Kintyre Way criss-crosses the peninsula, connecting communities and landscape, people and produce. At 89 miles long (142 kms), and with four to seven days worth of walking, there's serious hiking and gentle rambles, all of which bring home the beautiful reality that is Kintyre.

17 The West Island Way, which opened in September 2000, is the first long distance way-marked path on a Scottish island. It encompasses some of the best walking that the Isle of Bute has to offer and embraces a variety of landscapes.

18 The Cowal Way follows a route running the length of Argyll's Cowal Peninsula. It starts in the south west at Portavadie beside Loch Fyne, and finishes in the north east at Ardgartan by Loch Long, and involves walking on roads and on lochside, hill and woodland terrains. The waymarked route is 75 km / 47 miles in length and is divided into six shorter, more manageable sections.

VIEWS

19 Tiny Port Askaig on Islay is something of a ferry hub, serving Colonsay, the mainland and Jura. Its proximity to the last makes it an ideal location to view the Paps of Jura, three rounded mountains rising out of the sea to over 730m.

20 The village of Carradale on the eastern side of Kintyre makes an excellent base from which to explore the Peninsula. The delightful beach and harbour area offer stunning views over the Kilbrannan Sound to the dramatic hills of Arran.

21 One of Scotland's most romanticised stretches of water, the narrow straits known as the Kyles of Bute, more than live up to their reputation. The Kyles are best admired from the viewpoint on the A886 above Colintraive, where the view to their namesake island is truly awe-inspiring. Remember to bring along your picnic so you can really make the most of this view and open space.

22 The steep 10-minute climb from the centre of Oban to McCaig's Tower is well worth it for the view of Oban Bay, Kerrera and the Isle of Mull. The Tower was built by a local banker in the late 19th century in an effort to replicate Rome's Colosseum. The view of the town and the islands to the west is breathtaking.

68793

Argyll Caravan Park

Inveraray, Argyll, PA32 8XT
Tel:01499 302285 Fax:01499 302826
Email:enquiries@argyllcaravanpark.com
Web:www.argyllcaravanpark.com

50 acres, grassy, hardstanding, Apr-Oct.

Park accommodation: **270**

50 tourers £12.00-15.00, 50 motors £12.00-15.00. Total Touring Pitches 150.

5 Holiday Caravans to let, sleeps 4-6, £350.00 per week.

Leisure Facilities:

2½ mls S of Inveraray on the A83. Signposted.

21636

Mrs J MacDougall, Cuilreoch

Kilchrenan, Taynuilt, Argyll, PA35 1HG
Tel:01866 833236
Email:joyce@cuilreoch.freeserve.co.uk
Web:www.cuilreochcaravans.com

Mar-Oct.

Park accommodation: **2**

3 Holiday Caravans to let, sleeps 4-6, total sleeping capacity 16, £150.00-180.00 per week.

Leisure Facilities: From Glasgow/Edinburgh to Crianlarich - then A82 to Tyndrum; A85 to Taynuilt. Just before Taynuilt Village left on B845; bear right at Kilchrenan Inn; right at next junct; Cuilreoch ¼ ml on right. Signposted.

54387

David & Moira Gracie

Shieling Holidays, Craignure, Isle of Mull
PA65 6AY
Tel:01680 812496
Web:www.shielingholidays.co.uk (with email enquiry facility)

7 acres, mixed, Apr-Oct, extra charge for electricity, awnings. Rates per night from £14.00 (£12.00 no car).

Park accommodation: **90**

Stunning views over the sea to Ben Nevis. Family owners, small friendly and spotlessly clean. Super facilities, with lovely hot showers, hook-ups, laundry, dishwashing etc. Stroll to ferry, pub, bistro, steam railway and buses for Iona (for Staffa) and Tobermory, (for Ardnamurchan). Walk to golf, Torosay and Duart Castles. A perfect base for the whole island.

Leisure Facilities:

From the ferry, left on A849 to Iona. After 400 mts, left again and follow campsigns out to the sea. OS map 49 grid ref 724369. Signposted.

47704

North Ledaig Caravan Club Site

Connel, Oban, Argyll, PA37 1RU
Tel:01631 710291 Fax:01631 710520

Beautiful sea-shore location with breathtaking views to the islands. Conveniently situated near Oban it is an ideal base to relax, watch sunsets, enjoy watersports, explore local gardens and walk the nearby hills.

15 acres, grassy, hardstanding, Mar-Oct.

240 tourers/motor caravans £12.00-18.00 incl's mains hookup, 120 for Caravan Club members only.

From S on A85 in Connel turn L onto A828 and cross bridge (13½ ft). Site on L abt 1ml.

Park accommodation: **240**

Oban Harbour

IMPORTANT: PRICES STATED ARE ESTIMATES AND MAY BE SUBJECT TO AMENDMENTS
FOR A FULL LISTING OF QUALITY ASSURED CARAVAN AND CAMPING PARKS, PLEASE SEE DIRECTORY AT BACK OF THIS GUIDE

67

Canoeing on Loch Lomond, Argyll

Loch Lomond and The Trossachs

Whatever road you take to the bonny banks of Loch Lomond, you'll arrive at one of the most picturesque places in all of Scotland. This vast National Park is, indeed, one of the most beautiful places in the world.

Towns like Callander, Balloch, Killin and Aberfoyle make a great base to explore different corners of the Park. And once you're there, you'll find so much to do from watersports to mountain climbing, angling to gentle strolls in stunning locations.

You can even integrate the sedate with the active – catch the SS Sir Walter Scott from the Trossachs Pier and cruise Loch Katrine to Stronachlachar, then enjoy the 13-mile shore hike back.

The Falls of Dochart, Killin

DON'T MISS

1   **Loch Lomond and The Trossachs National Park** has its Gateway Centre on the southern shore of the Loch in Balloch. From here and elsewhere on the Loch, boat trips offer visitors the chance to explore the largest body of freshwater in Britain. To the west, Argyll Forest Park provides secluded waymarked trails, while The Trossachs to the east have provided inspiration for poets and novelists throughout the centuries.

2   The main visitor centre of the **Queen Elizabeth Forest Park** is on the A821 north of Aberfoyle. An integral part of the National Park, it offers a host of walking, wildlife and photography opportunities from the foot of Loch Lomond to Strathyre Forest, north of Loch Lubnaig. Here, you'll find a multitude of waymarked paths, a forest shop, wildlife viewing station and Liz MacGregor's Coffee Shop.

3   The dramatic scenery of The Trossachs is said to be the inspiration behind Sir Walter Scott's 'The Lady of the Lake'. It is fitting then that the historic steamship which regularly sets sail on Loch Katrine is named after him. The **SS Sir Walter Scott** cruises up to Stronachlachar and will return you to the Trossachs Pier.

4   At **Go Ape!** in Aberfoyle, you can take to the trees and experience a new, exhilarating course of rope bridges, tarzan swings and zip slides (including the longest in the UK) up to 37 metres above the forest floor. Approximately three hours of fun and adventure await.

5   For a fun family day out, visit the **Scottish Wool Centre** in Aberfoyle, where you can enjoy a light-hearted look at 2,000 years of Scottish history portrayed by human and animal actors, plus spinning and weaving demonstrations. The live animal show features sheepdogs rounding up both sheep and Indian Runner Ducks, whilst younger visitors can enjoy the lambs and baby goats in springtime.

FOOD AND DRINK

www.eatscotland.com

6　Whilst touring around Loch Lomond, be sure to stop at the Coach House Coffee Shop in the conservation village of Luss. Accompany a bumper homemade scone with a Lomond Latte or a Clyde Cappuccino!

7　The Village Inn at Arrochar is a charming country inn on the edge of Loch Long. Offering traditional Scottish home-cooking, it proves to be a great favourite with walkers exploring the adjacent 'Arrochar Alps'.

8　The family-friendly Forth Inn at Aberfoyle is known for its good food and atmosphere. Its award-winning bar and restaurant are favourites with locals and visitors alike.

9　The Kilted Skirlie is a modern Scottish restaurant with a sense of theatre that caters for every taste and pocket at Loch Lomond Shores, combine your visit with a range of shopping and leisure experiences and watch the otters at Loch Lomond Aquarium.

HISTORY AND HERITAGE

10　The islands of Loch Lomond are home to many ancient ruins including a 7th century monastery and the remains of a former Victorian whisky distillery.

11　The Lake of Menteith is the only 'lake' in Scotland, all others being known as lochs. Sail from the Port of Menteith, off the A81 south of Callander, to the island that is home to Inchmahome Priory, an 18th century Augustinian monastery.

12　The historic village of Killin, with the spectacular Falls of Dochart, is the setting for the Breadalbane Folklore Centre which is housed in a beautifully restored mill with a working waterwheel. Dedicated to exploring the rich myths and legends prevalent in these parts, you can follow the stories of the local clans and learn about St Fillan and the arrival of Christianity in Scotland. Open April to October.

VIEWS

13   The beauty of Loch Lomond is undisputed but the finest vantage point is more open to
      debate. Everyone has their favourite spot and no doubt you will too. Take a cruise on the Loch
      itself from Luss, Balloch or Tarbet or head to Inversnaid on the west bank for more rugged views.

14   'The Dumpling' is the nickname for Duncryne Hill, a volcanic plug, situated just off the A811 at
      the east end of Gartocharn. At about 465ft high and accessible by a short steep path, it is an
      astounding vantage point overlooking Loch Lomond's islands.

15   Conic Hill is located just north of Balmaha on the B837. A 358m ascent, it offers superb views
      of Loch Lomond and its islands. From here, you can also see the dramatic changes to the
      landscape caused by the Highland Boundary Fault.

16   From the Stronachlachar junction on the Inversnaid road (B829), the wild landscape of Loch
      Arklet leads down towards Loch Lomond and its surrounding hills.

WALKS   www.visitscotland.com/walking

17   To walk along the shore of Loch Katrine start at the Trossachs Pier, approximately 25 minutes drive
      west of Callander (A821). You can walk as far as you like and retrace your steps, or take a cruise on
      Loch Katrine to Stronachlachar and then walk the 13-mile route back to where you started.

18   The village hall in Balquhidder is your starting point for one of Breadalbane's most glorious views.
      Head along the Kirkton Burn and upwards onto a forest road. Soon you'll reach Creag an Tuirc
      where you can absorb the beauty of Balquhidder Glen, Loch Voil and little Loch Doine. Including a
      short climb, this 2½ mile walk should take you about 2 hours.

19   Rowardennan (B837 from Drymen) on the eastern edge of Loch Lomond is a wonderful starting
      and finishing point for a gentle walk along the shores, following part of the famous West Highland
      Way.

68185

Lomond Woods Holiday Park

Balloch, Loch Lomond, G83 8QP
Tel:01389 755000 Fax:01389 755563
Email:lomondwoods@holiday-parks.co.uk
Web:www.holiday-parks.co.uk

Family Holiday Park by Loch Lomond and the gateway to The,
National Park and Loch Lomond Shores visitor attraction. Pine
lodges and caravan holiday homes for hire and excellent facilities
for touring caravans. Open all year.

100 tourers £15.00-20.00, 100 motors £15.00-20.00. Total Touring
Pitches 100.

6 Holiday Caravans to let, sleeps 4-8, total sleeping capacity 30,
£200.00-550.00 per week.

Leisure Facilities:

17 mls N of Glasgow on A82 take a right to A811 Stirling route to
Balloch. Turn left at next r/about and first exit on r/about at
Macdonalds. Signposted.

Park accommodation: **200**

27321

Gart Caravan Park

Stirling Road, Callander, Perthshire, FK17 8LE
Tel/Fax:01877 330002
Email:enquiries@TheHolidayPark.co.uk
Web:www.TheHolidayPark.co.uk

grassy, level, sheltered, Apr-Oct, Extra charge for awnings.

128 tourers £15.00, Total Touring Pitches 128.

Leisure Facilities:

Situated on A84. From S park is 1ml before Callander town centre.
From N 1ml S of Callander.

Park accommodation: **210**

62150

Trossachs Holiday Park

Gartmore, Stirling, FK8 3SA
Tel:01877 382614 Fax:01877 382732
Email:info@trossachsholidays.co.uk
Web:www.trossachsholidays.co.uk

40 acres, in Scotland's National Park.

Tourers from £14.00-20.00, tents from £12.00-18.00.

Holiday Homes for hire, sleeps 1-6, from £239.00-549.00 per week.

Park accommodation: **165**

56909

Tyndrum, by Crianlarich, Perthshire   Map Ref: 1G2

Strathfillan Wigwams
Auchtertyre, Tyndrum, Perthshire, FK20 8RU
Tel:01838 400251
Email:wigwam@sac.ac.uk

Park accommodation: **25**

20 wooden wigwams, all with electric lighting/heating. Open all year.
New luxury wigwams with toilet/showers.

Scottish
TOURIST BOARD
★★★
CAMPING
PARK

Inversnaid, Loch Lomond

IMPORTANT: PRICES STATED ARE ESTIMATES AND MAY BE SUBJECT TO AMENDMENTS
FOR A FULL LISTING OF QUALITY ASSURED CARAVAN AND CAMPING PARKS, PLEASE SEE DIRECTORY AT BACK OF THIS GUIDE

73

Stirling Castle at dusk

Stirling and Forth Valley

Stirling and Forth Valley has a huge range of tourist attractions but one recent addition to the list is proving extremely popular. Built to celebrate the new Millennium and opened in 2002, The Falkirk Wheel is a triumph of engineering. It's the world's only rotating boat lift and, standing an impressive 24 metres high, it has reconnected the Forth & Clyde Canal with the Union Canal.

Scotland's industrial heritage is well represented locally at The Bo'ness and Kinneil Steam Railway, Birkhill Fireclay Mine and Callendar House, while you can see traces of Scotland's woollen industry on the opposite shores of the Forth in Clackmannan.

Around Stirling history is everywhere. Don't miss Stirling Castle and the Wallace Monument but remember to leave enough time to take a walk round the town and enjoy a spot of shopping too.

Port Street, Stirling

DON'T MISS

1. **Stirling Castle**, undoubtedly one of the finest in Scotland, sits high on its volcanic rock towering over the stunning countryside known as 'Braveheart Country'. A favourite royal residence over the centuries and a key military stronghold, see the Great Hall, the Chapel Royal, and the Renaissance Palace. From the Castle esplanade the sites of no less than seven historic battles can be seen, as can the majestic National Wallace Monument built in tribute to William Wallace.

2. The world's only rotating boatlift, **The Falkirk Wheel**, was constructed in 2002 to link the Forth & Clyde and Union canals. It is now possible for boats to traverse Central Scotland by canal for the first time in more than 40 years. Learn about Scotland's canal network in the visitor centre or board a vessel to take a trip on the mechanical marvel itself.

3. Just a few miles north west of Stirling on the A84 you will find **Blair Drummond Safari Park**. Here you can drive through wild animal reserves and get close to lions and zebras, and a whole host of other animals. Or you can park and walk around the pet farm, see the only elephants in Scotland, watch a sea lion display, find out what it's like to hold a bird of prey and take a boat to Chimp Island. There is also an adventure play area, pedal boats for hire and for the more adventurous – the flying fox!

4. Formerly known as 'Castle Gloom', **Castle Campbell** is beautifully sited at the head of Dollar Glen, immediately north of Dollar. Sitting in lofty isolation and overlooked by the Ochil Hills, the Castle became the chief Lowland stronghold of the Campbell clan, upon whose members the successive titles of Earl, Marquis and Duke of Argyll were bestowed. There are excellent walks through Dollar Glen to enjoy too.

FOOD AND DRINK

www.eatscotland.com

5   While in Stirling be sure to stop at the Portcullis Restaurant. Situated right next to the historic Stirling Castle the Portcullis was built in 1787 to serve the community as a school for boys. Today it offers a warm welcome, superb food, and a range of ales and wines, all served in cosy surroundings, complete with a real log fire in the winter months.

6   The lovely Victorian spa town of Bridge of Allan is home to the Bridge of Allan Brewery where you can see how traditional Scottish handcrafted ales are produced and even have a free tasting session!

7   Harviestoun Country Hotel & Restaurant in Tillicoultry is the perfect place to stop, whether it is for lunch, high tea or an evening meal. The restored 18th century steading, with the backdrop of the stunning Ochil Hills, is the ideal setting for relaxing with good food and fine wine.

HISTORY AND HERITAGE

8   Built in tribute to Scotland's national hero Sir William Wallace, the National Wallace Monument, by Stirling, can be seen for miles around. The Monument exhibition tells of William Wallace's epic struggle for a free Scotland.

9   On the site of the original battlefield, the Bannockburn Heritage Centre on the southern outskirts of Stirling, tells the story of the greatest victory of Scotland's favourite monarch King Robert the Bruce. Walk the battlefield and then enjoy the audio-visual presentation in the Centre, recounting the battle. A re-enactment of the battle takes place over two days every September.

10   Open the door to Callendar House in Falkirk, and you open the door to 600 years of Scottish history. Journey through time from the days of the Jacobites to the advent of the railway, and don't forget to stop at the Georgian kitchens for some refreshments prepared using authentic Georgian recipes.

11   The Tower Trail takes you for a tour around the amazing houses of the people who built Clackmannanshire - the 'Wee County'. These buildings show the changing fashion in tower building and are a great survival of the heritage of medieval Scotland, built by the families who shaped the later industrial development of the county.

12   Situated by the banks of the River Teith, Doune Castle was once the ancestral home of the Earls of Moray. At one time occupied by the Jacobite troops, this castle can now be explored and makes a great picnic spot.

WALKS

13 **The Antonine Wall** dates back to the 2nd century and once marked the northern frontier of the Roman Empire. Substantial lengths have been preserved and can still be seen at various sites around Falkirk. Follow the wall for a relaxing walk along the towpath on the north of the canal, taking you past the Falkirk Wheel to Bonnybridge.

14 Not far from Dollar where the A823 meets the A977 it's worth stopping to explore the delightful **Rumbling Bridge**, so named because of the continuous rumbling sound of the falls and the river below. The unusual double bridge spans a narrow gorge and you'll find a network of platforms and paths that take you over the river and deep into the gorge with spectacular views of waterfalls and swirling pools.

15 At the heart of Clackmannanshire's 300-acre **Gartmorn Dam Country Park**, visitors can enjoy a short walk with gentle gradients suitable for wheelchairs or pushchairs. Gartmorn Dam is the oldest man-made reservoir still in use in Scotland, and is a nature reserve which is the winter home of thousands of migratory ducks.

16 The **Darn Walk** from Bridge of Allan to Dunblane is a beautiful walk which can be enjoyed at any time of the year. Highlights include a scenic stretch alongside the River Allan and the cave which was Robert Louis Stevenson's inspiration for Ben Gunn's cave in Treasure Island. The walk can be completed in 1½ to 2 hours.

ATTRACTIONS

17 Savour the evocative sights, sounds and smells of a nostalgic railway journey aboard the **Bo'ness & Kinneil Steam Train**. Your journey will take you to the cavernous Birkhill Fireclay Mine where you can learn about the 300 year old fossils of giant tree ferns.

18 Plenty of fun, with laughs and thrills in equal measure, **Stirling Old Town Jail** presents life in an authentic Victorian prison. You'll see wardens, prisoners and governors, and might even meet the notorious hangman! When you're finished, head across to the Tolbooth, the former city jail. Today, it's a vibrant music and arts venue with a superb bistro and restaurant.

19 Just north of Stirling, **Argaty Red Kites** is Scotland's only red kite feeding station. After 130 years Scottish Natural Heritage and the RSPB have reintroduced these exciting, acrobatic birds to central Scotland. Spend a day and you can enjoy a guided walk or just watch the birds from the hide.

The Queen's View, Perthshire

PERTHSHIRE, ANGUS AND DUNDEE AND THE KINGDOM OF FIFE

Scotland's heartlands are the perfect holiday destination in many ways. There's so much to discover in this part of the world that you're sure to find something that suits you perfectly. Golfing, fishing, walking, sightseeing, there's an abundance of choice and there are some wonderful places to stay.

There's an excellent selection of touring and holiday parks in the area – many with exceptional facilities like swimming pools, games rooms, play areas and even salmon and trout fishing on site!

The countryside is so varied too. Fife has an enviable coastline with a number of perfect little harbour towns, Perthshire is unspoiled and magnificent, with some of Scotland's finest woodlands and stunning lochs and hills. And then there's Dundee – the area's largest city. There's always another fascinating place waiting to be explored.

This is a holiday destination that can be as active as you want it to be. For the outdoor enthusiast, there's anything from hill walking to whitewater rafting and pretty much everything in between. Anglers love the thrill of pursuing salmon and trout on some of the country's greatest river beats or heading out to sea where the catch can be bountiful.

Golfers love this area too – some of the world's finest courses are here from the home of golf at St Andrews to championship quality greats like Gleneagles and Carnoustie, host of last year's Open.

If wildlife's your thing, there are many wonderful sights to see. In the countryside of Perthshire and the Angus Glens there are ospreys, eagles, otters, red squirrels and deer. By the sea from Fife to Angus there are opportunities to spot a wide variety of seabirds – especially around the Montrose Basin which attracts thousands of migrant species.

You don't have to be escaping civilisation to enjoy these parts, however. There are towns and cities that you'll enjoy enormously, each with their own unique attractions. Perth has specialist shops and high street retailers. St Andrews is a fine university town with a fascinating history. Dunfermline was once the seat of Scotland's Kings while Dundee, the City of Discovery is enjoying something of a renaissance these days and is a great place for a big day out.

Church Square, St Andrews, Fife

Dundee Contemporary Arts Centre, Dundee

What's On?

Snowdrop Festival 2008
1 February – 16 March 2008
www.visitscotland.com/snowdrops

StAnza 2008, St Andrews
13 – 16 March 2008
www.stanzapoetry.org

Perth Festival of the Arts
22 May - 1 June 2008
www.perthfestival.co.uk

Angus Glens Walking Festival
29 May - 1 June 2008
www.angusanddundee.co.uk/
walkingfestival

Dundee Blues Bonanza
27 - 29 June 2008
www.dundeebluesbonanza.co.uk

Game Conservancy Scottish Fair, Scone Palace
4 - 6 July 2008
www.scottishfair.com

The Big Tent 2008: Scotland's Festival of Stewardship, Falkland
26 – 27 July 2008
www.bigtentfestival.co.uk

Pittenweem Arts Festival
2 – 10 August 2008
www.pittenweemartsfestival.co.uk

Blair Castle International Horse Trials, Blair Atholl
21-24 August 2008
www.blairhorsetrials.co.uk

Dundee Flower and Food Festival, Camperdown Park
5 - 7 September 2008
www.dundeeflowerand
foodfestival.com

Angus and Dundee Roots Festival
6 -13 September 2008
www.tayroots.com

The Enchanted Forest, Faskally Wood, by Pitlochry
17 October – 2 November 2008
www.enchantedforest.org.uk

www.perthshire.co.uk
www.angusanddundee.co.uk
www.visitfife.com

All dates correct at time of publication. Please check before booking. VisitScotland cannot be held responsible for any inaccuracies.

79

MAP

©Collins Bartholomew Ltd 2007

TOURIST INFORMATION CENTRES

Perthshire	
Aberfeldy	The Square, Aberfeldy PH15 2DD
Blairgowrie	26 Wellmeadow, Blairgowrie PH10 6AS
Crieff	High Street, Crieff PH7 3HU
Dunkeld	The Cross, Dunkeld PH8 0AN
Perth	Lower City Mills, West Mill Street, Perth PH1 5QP
Pitlochry	22 Atholl Road, Pitlochry PH16 5BX
Angus and Dundee	
Arbroath	Harbour Visitor Centre, Fishmarket Quay, Arbroath DD11 1PS
Brechin	Brechin Castle Centre, Haughmuir, Brechin DD9 6RL
Dundee	21 Castle Street, Dundee DD1 3AA
Fife	
Dunfermline	1 High Street, Dunfermline KY12 7DL
Kirkcaldy	The Merchant's House, 339 High Street, Kirkcaldy KY1 1JL
St Andrews	70 Market Street, St Andrews KY16 9NU

Make the most of your stay in Scotland and make your first stop the Tourist Information Centre wherever you go.

Knowledgeable and friendly staff can help you with information and advice; they can answer your questions, book accommodation and you can even pick up some souvenirs to take home for friends and family.

For information and ideas about exploring Scotland in advance of your trip, call our booking and information service or go to **www.visitscotland.com**

Call 0845 22 55 121

or if calling from outside the UK call **+44 (0) 1506 832 121**

From Ireland call **1800 932 510**

A £4 booking fee applies to telephone bookings of accommodation.

Scottish Crannog Centre, Kenmore, Loch Tay

Perthshire

Perthshire is one of the most strikingly picturesque parts of Scotland. It ranges from the wild and mountainous to sophisticated and cultured; from the wilderness of Rannoch Moor to the lap of luxury at the 5-star Gleneagles Hotel.

You can experience everything in Perthshire from traditional activities like golf, fishing and field sports to more recent innovations like sphereing and white water rafting. Whatever activities you pursue, it will be against a backdrop of spectacular scenery; high mountains, deep forests, sparkling lochs and wide rivers.

But you don't have to spend the day pushing yourself to the limits, a walk through Perthshire's wonderful woodlands may suffice. Or you could take a romantic stroll around the Birks of Aberfeldy, visit some of Britain's most colourful gardens, marvel at a reconstructed Iron Age crannog on Loch Tay or simply enjoy the Queen's View near Pitlochry.

The Famous Grouse Experience, Crieff

DON'T MISS

1   The **Scottish Crannog Centre** at Kenmore on Loch Tay is an authentic recreation of an ancient loch-dwelling. Imagine a round house in the middle of a loch with a thatched roof, on stilts. You can tour the Crannog to see how life used to be 2,600 years ago. Upon your return to shore, have a go at a variety of Iron Age crafts; see if you can grind the grain, drill through stone or make fire through wood friction.

2   **Scone Palace**, near Perth, was renowned as the traditional crowning palace of Scottish kings, as the capital of the Pictish kingdom and centre of the ancient Celtic Church. Nowadays, the great house and its beautiful accompanying grounds are home to the Earls of Mansfield, and offer an ideal day out.

3   **Blair Castle**, the stunningly situated ancient seat of the Dukes and Earls of Atholl, is a 5-star castle experience. The unmistakeable white façade is visible from the A9 just north of Blair Atholl. Dating back 740 years, the Castle has played a part in some of Scotland's most tumultuous events but today is a relaxing and fascinating place.

4   **The Famous Grouse Experience** is housed within Glenturret, Scotland's oldest malt whisky distillery. It is an interactive attraction where visitors can familiarise themselves with this renowned tipple and the brand that accompanies it! As well as a tour of the production areas, you can enjoy a unique audio-visual presentation which gives a grouse's eye view of Scotland.

5   Among its many other attractions, Perthshire – known as **Big Tree Country** - can boast some of the most remarkable trees and woodlands anywhere in Europe. Its forests, woods and country gardens offer an unsurpassed assortment of glorious greenery that is home to many different species of wildlife. Here you'll discover Europe's oldest tree in Fortingall Churchyard, the world's highest hedge and one of Britain's tallest trees at The Hermitage by Dunkeld.

6   Enjoy the renowned **Queen's View** by Loch Tummel. Although a favourite spot of Queen Victoria it was actually named after Isabella, wife of King Robert the Bruce. The viewpoint is well signposted from the A9 just north of Pitlochry and there is a fascinating visitor centre and café.

FOOD AND DRINK
www.eatscotland.com

7   Farmers' markets have seen something of resurgence in recent years in the UK and **Perth's Farmers' Market** is arguably the best know in Scotland. Taking place throughout the year on the first Saturday of each month, it is a showcase for local producers and growers. Look out for fish, meat and game, baked goods, fruit wines and liqueurs, honeys and preserves, fruit and vegetables, sweets and herbs.

8   The area around Blairgowrie is Europe's centre for soft fruit production and a particular feature of the area are the signs at farms inviting you to 'pick your own' strawberries, raspberries, gooseberries, redcurrants, and tayberries. Sample the local produce at **Cairn o' Mohr Wines** in Errol. A family-run business it produces truly unique Scottish fruit wines. Explore the winery and have a tasting session!

9   **Edradour Distillery** – Scotland's smallest malt whisky distillery - can be found in the Highland foothills just to the east of Pitlochry. Built in the early 19th century Edradour is the only remaining 'farm' distillery in Perthshire and sometimes it seems to have hardly changed in 170 years. Enjoy a guided tour and relax with a wee dram.

10 **Gloagburn Farm Shop and Restaurant** at Tibbermore near Perth is a rare gem of a food stop. A great menu is created from local produce, as much as possible reared or grown at the farm itself. The sandwiches and soup are superb and nutritious, or treat yourself to some of the mouth-watering cakes. Stock up on your way out at the farm shop.

WALKS
www.visitscotland.com/walking

11 The 63-mile circular **Cateran Trail**, through Perthshire and the Angus Glens, follows paths used by 15th century Caterans (cattle rustlers). Complete the whole route in a leisurely five days or enjoy a shorter section on a day's walk. Take in the soft contours of Strathardle on the Bridge of Cally to Kirkmichael section or head for the hills between Kirkmichael and the Spittal of Glenshee.

12 Revered in poetry by the national bard, Robert Burns, the **Birks of Aberfeldy** ('birks' being the old Scots for birch trees) line a short walk alongside the Moness Burn, reached from Aberfeldy town centre or a car park on the Crieff Road. A circular path leads to a beautiful waterfall, where birds and flowers are abundant.

13 **Killiecrankie**, just north of Pitlochry, is known for two reasons – the famous battle in 1689 and its status as a Site of Special Scientific Interest. The visitor centre has a seasonal interactive wildlife display and, together with the café and shop, makes for an interesting stop.

14 On the A9, 1 mile west of Dunkeld, you'll find **The Hermitage**. A beautiful walk along the banks of the River Braan takes you to the focal point, Ossian's Hall set in a picturesque gorge and overlooking Black Linn Falls. Ask the local rangers for advice or read the display panels as you pass amidst the huge Douglas Firs en route.

WILDLIFE

www.visitscotland.com/wildlife

15 **Loch Leven National Nature Reserve**, near Kinross, incorporates the largest loch in Lowland Scotland and is one of the most important sites for waterfowl in Britain. It attracts the largest concentration of breeding ducks in the UK, and many thousands of migratory ducks, geese and swans. Start your visit at RSPB Vane Farm which has excellent observation hides.

16 Visit **Loch of the Lowes** between April and August and there's every chance you'll encounter its famous nesting ospreys. The Scottish Wildlife Trust's visitor centre provides interpretation on the birds, which migrate to Scotland from their winter homes in West Africa. There are also telescopes and binoculars on hand to give you a better view. Between October and March, the nature reserve is worth visiting for the sheer numbers of wildfowl.

17 **Blair Castle Deer Park**, located in the grounds of Blair Castle, has a small herd of native red deer including an impressive stag. Red squirrels, a species now rare in many parts of Britain, are also a common sight in the woods around Atholl Estates. For a good chance of seeing one try the mile-long Red Squirrel Trail starting from Glen Tilt car park.

18 Each year between April and October an average of 5,400 salmon fight their way upstream and must by-pass the Hydro-Electric Dam at Pitlochry by travelling through the interconnected pools that form the **Pitlochry 'fish ladder'**. Witness it all at a very special attraction.

ADVENTURE

www.visitscotland.com/adventure

In this area you'll find over 35 different adventure activities! Here's a selection:

19 Perthshire is renowned for its stunning lochs and rivers, many of which are excellent for **white water rafting**. A truly unforgettable experience awaits you with a spectacular combination of rugged Highland scenery and the adrenaline rush of this activity. Get some friends together and go for it!

20 Perthshire is the only place in Scotland where you can try **sphereing**. It involves a huge 12ft inflatable ball which the willing participants strap themselves safely into and then take a wild and bouncy tumble down the hill. This one already has thrill seekers and outdoor enthusiasts queuing up!

21 Wet, wild and wonderful - **canyoning** is all this and more! Unleash your adrenaline streak as you swim through rapids, cliff jump into deep clear pools, abseil through waterfalls and slide down natural stone 'flumes'. This one is awesome and not to be missed!

22 If you enjoy wide-open spaces try a **microlight** flight for the nearest experience to flying like a bird. With the latest microlight technology, enjoy up to 60 miles of spectacular views and scenery in one hour. This is a great way to enjoy the Perthshire landscape as well as being the experience of a lifetime.

23 Try to imagine descending fast whitewater in a cross between a raft and an armchair armed with your wet suit, bouyancy aid, helmet, and hand and feet flippers ... the reality is **river bugging** and participants are called 'buggers' so strap in, sit back and go crazy!

15365

Blair Atholl, Perthshire   Map Ref: 4C12

Blair Castle Caravan Park

Blair Atholl, Perthshire, PH18 5SR
Tel:01796 481263 Fax:01796 481587
Email:mail@blaircastlecaravanpark.co.uk
Web:www.blaircastlecaravanpark.co.uk

32 acres, mixed, Mar-Nov. Extra charge for electricity, awnings.

150 tourers £14.00-17.00, 68 tents £14.00-17.00. Total Touring Pitches 270.

27 Holiday Caravans to let, sleeps 4-6, £210.00-495.00 per week.

Leisure Facilities: ● ✪

32 mls N of Perth, just off main A9 (Perth-Inverness road)

Park accommodation: 385

15401

Blairgowrie, Perthshire   Map Ref: 2B1

Blairgowrie Holiday Park

Blairgowrie, Perthshire, PH10 7AL
Tel:01250 876666 Fax:01250 874535
Email:blairgowrie@holiday-parks.co.uk
Web:www.holiday-parks.co.uk

Family Holiday Park set in beautiful landscaped grounds. Pine Lodges and Thistle Award Caravan Holiday Homes for hire. Touring caravans welcome.

19 tourers £13.00-15.00, 2 motors £13.00-15.00. Total Touring Pitches 24.

6 Holiday Caravans to let, sleeps 4-8, total sleeping capacity 42, £175.00-430.00 per week.

Follow A93 N from Blairgowrie town centre. Approx 1ml turn right at caravan park signs. Park is 300 yds on left. Signposted.

Park accommodation: 170

20529

Bridge of Cally, Perthshire   Map Ref: 2B1

Corriefodly Holiday Park

Bridge of Cally, PH10 7JG
Tel:01250 876666 Fax:01250 874535
Email:corriefodly@holiday-parks.co.uk
Web:www.holiday-parks.co.uk

Riverside family Holiday Park sheltered by hills and woodland in the heart of Perthshire countryside. Open Jan-Dec.

20 tourers £12.00-15.00, 20 motors £12.00-15.00. Total Touring Pitches 20.

3 Holiday Caravans to let, sleeps 4-6, total sleeping capacity 18, £170.00-375.00 per week.

Leisure Facilities: ● ✪

From Blairgowrie follow A93 for 6 mls to village of Bridge of Cally. Take left at post office over bridge (signed Pitlochry). Park is 200 yds on left. Signposted.

Park accommodation: 130

PERTHSHIRE

63689

Comrie, Perthshire | Map Ref: 2A2

West Lodge Caravan Park

Comrie, Perthshire, PH6 2LS
Tel/Fax:01764 670354
Web:www.westlodgecaravanpark.co.uk

3.5 acres, grassy, sheltered, Apr-Oct. Extra charge for awnings.

Park accommodation: 50 ⛺🚐🚐🏠Å🚍

10 tourers/motorhomes £15.00-24.00, tents £10.00-20.00. Total Touring Pitches 10.

6 Holiday Caravans to let, sleeps 4-6, total sleeping capacity 34, £200.00-275.00 per week (nightly £35.00-45.00).

A85 between Crieff & Comrie. 1ml E of Comrie. Signposted.

16071

Crieff, Perthshire | Map Ref: 2A2

Braidhaugh Park

South Bridgend, Crieff, Perthshire, PH7 4DH
Tel:01764 652951   Fax:01764 652692
Email:info@braidhaugh.co.uk
Web:www.braidhaugh.co.uk

Close to Crieff town centre, static and tourers. Jan-Dec. Extra charge for awnings.

3 Holiday Homes to let, sleeps 2-4.

Park accommodation: 110 ⛺🚐🚐🏠

38495

Pitlochry, Perthshire | Map Ref: 2A1

Milton of Fonab Caravan Site

Bridge Road, Pitlochry, Perthshire, PH16 5NA
Tel:01796 472882 Fax:01796 474363
Email:info@fonab.co.uk
Web:www.fonab.com

15 acres, grassy, level, Mar-Oct, Extra charge for awnings.

Park accommodation: 210 ⛺🏠Å🚍

164 tourers/motorhomes £14.50-20.50, 10 tents £14.50-17.00, Total Touring Pitches 174.

36 Holiday Caravans to let, sleeps 6, total sleeping capacity 216, £240.00-430.00 per week.

½ ml S of Pitlochry opposite Bell's Distillery on Pitlochry Festival, Theatre road. Signposted.

75824

by Pitlochry, Perthshire | Map Ref: 2A1

Glengoulandie Country Park

By Pitlochry, Perthshire, PH16 5NL
Tel:01887 830495

Camping (20 pitches with facilities), Deer Park, Fly-fishing lochan, Coffee Shop and small kid's play area.

Park accommodation: 60 ⛺🚐Å

IMPORTANT: PRICES STATED ARE ESTIMATES AND MAY BE SUBJECT TO AMENDMENTS
FOR A FULL LISTING OF QUALITY ASSURED CARAVAN AND CAMPING PARKS, PLEASE SEE DIRECTORY AT BACK OF THIS GUIDE

87

RRS Discovery at Discovery Point, Dundee

Angus and Dundee

The Angus and Dundee area boasts beautiful beaches and coastline – wonderful unspoiled stretches of sand which are, at times windswept and stormy but more frequently, warm and inviting, with the peace only occasionally shattered by the cries of the seabirds.

Dundee, you'll discover, has a proud maritime history. Captain Scott's polar research ship the RRS Discovery has returned to the city that built it and is now a top tourist attraction. The city's industrial past also features high on the tourist trail – don't miss the Verdant Works (a former winner of Europe's Top Industrial Museum award) where you

can learn about the jute trade that was once a mainstay of the city's economy.

For a complete contrast to city life, explore the Angus Glens. There are five: Glen Isla, Glen Prosen, Glen Lethnot, Glen Clova and Glen Esk. Each has its own unique features but all of the Glens are exceptionally beautiful and wonderfully peaceful places to explore.

Lunan Bay, Angus

DON'T MISS

1   Perhaps Scotland's finest fairytale castle, Glamis Castle is famed for its Macbeth connections, as well as being the birthplace of the late Princess Margaret and childhood home of the late Queen Mother. Set against the backdrop of the Grampian Mountains, Glamis is an L-shaped castle built over 5-storeys in striking pink sandstone. The grounds host the Grand Scottish Proms the second week in August each year, complete with spectacular fireworks display.

2   Little more than half an hour's drive north of the bustling city of Dundee, a series of picturesque valleys runs north into the heart of the Grampians. Collectively known as the Angus Glens, they offer the perfect escape for those seeking a walk, a spot of wildlife watching, a scenic picnic or a pub lunch. Ranging from gentle and wooded (Glen Isla) to the truly awe-inspiring (Glen Clova and neighbouring Glen Doll), there is more to discover here than you can fit into a single trip.

3   Discover Dundee's polar past at Discovery Point. Step aboard Captain Scott's famous ship that took Scott and Shackleton to Antarctica in 1901 and come face to face with the heroes of the ice in the award-winning visitor centre.

4   Dundee is the perfect place for a city break, with great shopping, restaurants and nightlife. Spend a day in Dundee's vibrant and cool Cultural Quarter where you can indulge in speciality shopping at the Westport; visit Sensation Dundee's Science Centre which explores the world of the senses; take in a film or an exhibition at Dundee Contemporary Arts; visit Dundee's acclaimed Rep Theatre; and round it all off with a meal at one of the many restaurants and a drink at one of the area's contemporary bars.

5   For the chance to see bottlenose dolphins at close proximity, why not book a trip on one of the River Tay Dolphin Trips. If you prefer to stay on dry land the dolphins can sometimes be seen from Broughty Ferry Beach.

6   Angus was the heartland of the Picts, a warrior people who lived in Scotland around 2,000 years ago and left behind many intriguing monuments. Pictavia, in Brechin, provides a fascinating insight including hands-on exhibits and a themed play area for all the family. The small hamlet of Aberlemno, 6 miles north east of Forfar, is famous for its intricately sculptured Pictish cross-slab in the churchyard.

FOOD AND DRINK

www.eatscotland.com

7   The But 'n Ben in Auchmithie, just 5 miles north of Arbroath, is one of the best seafood restaurants in the area and serves as its speciality the 'smokie pancake'.

8   Jute Café Bar is situated on the ground floor of Dundee Contemporary Arts centre with panoramic river views. Its menu ranges widely, with the emphasis on informality, while the ambience goes from a relaxing morning coffee venue to a stylish evening hotspot. Eat, drink and enjoy yourself with freshly cooked dishes, everything from a light snack to a full meal.

9   The Roundhouse Restaurant at Lintrathen, by Kirriemuir, is an award-winning restaurant offering innovative modern menus using Angus and Perthshire produce in a peaceful rural setting. The chef is a former Master Chef of Great Britain, whose specialities include local Angus beef and game.

10   No visit to the area would be complete without stopping off to pick up some of the area's best local produce to take home. Milton Haugh Farm Shop specialises in the freshest seasonal potatoes, own-reared beef and free range chickens. The Corn Kist Coffee Shop also serves up some delicious home made meals and tempting treats.

WALKS

www.visitscotland.com/walking

11   Scenic Glen Doll is one of the famous Angus Glens, north of Dundee. Follow one of the waymarked forest walks from the car park, or more ambitious hikers can take any of three rights of way leading over the surrounding hills into the neighbouring valleys of Glen Shee and Royal Deeside.

12   Situated five miles north west of Carnoustie, Crombie Country Park covers 100 hectares of mixed woodland around a picturesque reservoir. There are great opportunities for wildlife watching including butterflies, water and woodland birds.

13   Seaton Cliffs Nature Trail is a self guided trail which goes from Arbroath into Sites of Special Scientific Interest, and the sea cliffs are spectacular. There are 15 interpretative points of interest and a wide variety of seabird species can be seen including puffins, guillemots, razorbill and eider duck to name but a few. Allow approximately 2 hours and 30 minutes.

14   If you want to get out and about in the fresh air, see some of what Dundee has to offer, and get fit at the same time, why not try out one of the themed Dundee city centre walks in the Dundee Walking Guide available from the Tourist Information Centre. The trails include buildings of historical significance, examples of both 19th and 20th century architecture, plus explorations of Dundee's maritime and industrial heritage, and along the routes you will pass many of Dundee's visitor attractions where you can take a break.

GOLF

www.visitscotland.com/golf

15 If you want to experience the very best in Scottish golf, a visit to the Carnoustie Championship Course is a must. Venue for the 2007 Open Golf Championship, the course has been deemed the 'toughest links course in the world'.

16 Montrose Medal Golf Course, established in 1562, is the fifth oldest golf course in the world with a traditional links layout.

17 Downfield Golf Club is an attractive parkland course that has played host to many golfing tournaments and has an excellent reputation as a challenging course.

18 Kirriemuir Golf Course is a gem of a parkland course designed by the renowned James Braid. Look out for the notorious oak tree at the 18th!

HISTORY AND HERITAGE

19 JM Barrie's Birthplace at Kirriemuir has been carefully restored to reflect how it might have looked in the 1860s. The exhibition next door details the life and work of this hugely talented and celebrated author, famous for writing Peter Pan.

20 In 1178 William the Lion founded the now ruined Tironensian monastery that is Arbroath Abbey, near the harbour in Arbroath. The Abbey is famously associated with the Declaration of Arbroath, signed here in 1320, which asserted Scotland's independence from England. An adjacent visitor centre tells the building's story.

21 Edzell Castle is an elegant 16th century residence with tower house that was home to the Lindsays. The beautiful walled garden was created by Sir David Lindsay in 1604 and features an astonishing architectural framework. The 'Pleasance' is a delightful formal garden with walls decorated with sculptured stone panels, flower boxes and niches for nesting birds.

The golf course at Aberdour, Fife

Kingdom of Fife

If you're a golfer, the ancient Kingdom of Fife will be a powerful draw. Every serious golfer wants to play the Old Course at St Andrews at least once in a lifetime and, thanks to a public allocation of rounds each day, you can. There are also over 40 other fabulous courses in Fife to put your game to the test.

For keen walkers, one of the great ways to explore Fife is on foot. The Fife Coastal Path takes in some truly delightful places and you'll get to relax on some of the best beaches in the country – with four Fife beaches achieving the top standard Blue Flag status in 2007.

Fife's seaside communities have their roots in fishing and the North Sea herring fleet used to land its catch in the East Neuk's ports. The harbour's still busy at Anstruther but the halcyon days of deep sea fishing have been consigned to the fascinating exhibitions in the Scottish Fisheries Museum in the town.

Dunfermline Abbey, Fife

DON'T MISS

1   A prosperous university town and Mecca for golfers from across the planet, St Andrews is one
    of Scotland's top attractions. Situated above two of the country's finest sandy beaches, there is a
    real medieval feel to the town's cobbled streets and closes, reinforced by the presence of a ruined
    cathedral dating from 1180 and a castle founded around 1200. Notwithstanding the many golf
    courses to pick from, you may also wish to visit the local Aquarium or Botanic Garden.

2   Dunfermline's royal and monastic past dominates the town. This former capital of Scotland,
    birthplace of James I and Charles I, boasts a royal palace, a 12th century abbey and is the final
    resting place of King Robert the Bruce and eleven other Scottish Kings and Queens. King Malcolm
    Canmore established his court after the death of Macbeth at the now ruined fortified tower in the
    heart of "The Glen" – the extensive and picturesque Pittencrieff Park – gifted to the people of
    Dunfermline by local philanthropist Andrew Carnegie.

3   Travel through the quaint fishing villages of the East Neuk of Fife and you travel back through
    time. This corner of Fife is filled with traditional cottages with red pantile roofs and crow-stepped
    gable ends which appear unchanged from a bygone age. Fishing boats lie at rest in the harbours
    following the bustle of unloading their catch. Between communities lie unspoilt stretches of sandy
    beach, perfect for walks and picnics. Visit Pittenweem for art, Crail for crafts or Anstruther for a trip
    to the Isle of May, followed by some of Britain's finest fish and chips.

4   To wander through the narrow cobbled streets of the Royal Burgh of Culross is to
    experience life from a past time. Meander through the cobbled streets skirting the shoreline of the
    Firth of Forth, overlooked by the red pantiled roofs of the harled whitewashed cottages. Now in the
    care of the National Trust for Scotland – this is without doubt the finest and most complete
    example of a 17th and 18th century Scottish town.

FOOD AND DRINK

www.eatscotland.com

5   **The Inn at Lathones**, near St Andrews, is a coaching inn with a history stretching back 400 years. The restaurant here continues to welcome travellers with a tempting menu featuring the best of local produce transformed into à la carte gourmet delights.

6   The renowned **Peat Inn**, 3 miles from Cupar, offers top quality modern Scottish cuisine. Only the very best of local produce is used and dishes are prepared with great skill and flair. A mouth-watering wine list is available and visitors wishing to sleep off a hearty meal can stay over in the indulgent 5-star accommodation.

7   **Balbirnie House**, a Georgian mansion set in its own 416-acre country estate, is recognised as one of Scotland's finest Grade A listed historic houses. Dining in either the Orangery or the Balbirnie Bistro provides a delightful way to experience the natural larder that Scotland has to offer and both have built up a deserved reputation as two of the best restaurants in Fife.

8   **Cardoon** at Best Western Keavil House offers a varied menu of light dishes to modern Scottish dishes using locally sourced, quality food, which is served in a relaxed and stylish setting. Experience mouth-watering food and excellent service in this award-winning restaurant – one of Fife's dining gems.

BEACHES AND GOLF

9   Fife boasts some of Scotland's finest and cleanest sandy beaches, great for peaceful strolls or quiet contemplation. The area is home to four of Scotland's five Blue Flag award-winning strands at Aberdour, Burntisland, Elie, and West Sands, St Andrews – each offering magnificent views and wonderful experiences.

10 Recognised worldwide as the Home of Golf – the Old Course in St Andrews is where it all began and it still remains a real test for today's champions. To play on these hallowed fairways and greens is a dream come true for the golfing fan and an experience which will not be forgotten.

11 As well as the iconic Old Course – the small peninsula of the Kingdom of Fife boasts over 40 other wonderful golf courses each offering something different for the visiting golfer. Try the testing challenges of the Open Qualifying courses or an enjoyable, relaxing game, links or parkland, 9 or 18 hole – golf is a way of life in the Kingdom of Fife and there is something for everyone.

12 The sand dunes and beach at the mouth of the Tay estuary are one of the fastest growing parts of Scotland and home to Tentsmuir – one of Scotland's National Nature Reserves. This dynamic coastline is important for waders and wildfowl, common and grey seals, ducks and seaduck, and colourful butterflies that light up the grassland and dunes in summer. It is truly one of Scotland's most magical coastlines and well worth a visit.

WALKING AND WILDLIFE

13   Stretching around much of Fife's coastline from the Royal Burgh of Culross to the Tay Bridge, the Fife Coastal Path can be experienced in short bite-sized walks or as a long distance route to bring your senses to life. Listen to the seabirds soaring above the waves, smell the salt sea air and savour the sea breezes on this wonderful stretch of coast.

14   The Isle of May, accessible via the May Princess from Anstruther in spring and summer, provides nesting sites for 200,000 seabirds, including over 100,000 puffins between May and July alone. In autumn, thousands of grey seals come ashore here to pup.

15   Dominating the skyline of central Fife, the Lomond Hills are one of the area's most popular walking destinations. The regional park which encompasses the hills extends over 65 square miles and provides ample opportunity for both moderate and more challenging walking experiences with spectacular vistas over the surrounding countryside.

16   The Scottish Deer Centre, near Cupar, allows visitors to spot nine species of deer in over 55 acres of scenic parkland as well as its very own pack of wolves. There are daily falconry displays featuring native Scottish species, a range of shops and a cosy café.

HERITAGE AND GARDENS

17   The Scottish Fisheries Museum in Anstruther is a multi-award winning national museum which tells the story of Scottish fishing and whaling from the earliest times to the present – bringing the sea-faring heritage of the people of the Fife coast to life.

18   The Royal Palace of Falkland was the countryside residence of Stuart Kings and Queens when they hunted deer and wild boar in the forests of Fife, and was a favourite childhood playground of Mary, Queen of Scots. The Palace was built in the 1500s by James IV and James V, replacing an earlier castle from the 12th century. The current spacious garden, dating from the mid-20th century, houses the original Royal Tennis Court – the oldest in Britain still in use – built in 1539.

19   Cambo Gardens is a romantic 'Secret Garden' nestled on the coast between St Andrews and the East Neuk of Fife. Created around Cambo Burn the garden boasts everything from spectacular snowdrops to glowing autumn borders, a wild array of woodland plants and animals, waterfalls and rose-clad wrought-iron bridges. This truly is a plantsman's paradise.

20   Aberdour Castle was built by the Douglas family in the 13th century and has been added to throughout the centuries to create a wonderful mix of styles. Situated in the delightful village of the same name, Aberdour Castle boasts fine interior painted ceilings, galleries, a beehive shaped doocot as well as a delightful walled garden only recently uncovered.

41599

Sauchope Links Park

Crail, Fife, KY10 3XJ
Tel:01333 450460 Fax:01333 450246
Email:info@sauchope.co.uk
Web:www.sauchope.co.uk

23 acres, grassy, level, Mar-Oct, Extra charge for awnings.

Total Touring Pitches 50.

4 Holiday Caravans to let, sleeps 4-6, total sleeping capacity 20.

Leisure Facilities:

From St Andrews take A918 to Crail. Enter village, at sharp right hand corner turn left. Park signposted 400 yds on right.

Park accommodation: 150

66475

Kingdom Caravan Park

1 Overstenton Farm, Glenrothes, Fife, KY6 2NG
Tel/Fax:01592 772226
Email:t.mcallister2@btinternet.com

Newly developed site close to local attractions.

Park accommodation: 64

Static caravans for hire, sleeps upto 6. Rates from £200.00-300.00.

35332

Letham Feus Caravan Park

Cupar Road, By Lundin Links, Fife, KY8 4NT
Tel:01333 351900
Email:info@largoleisure.co.uk
Web:www.largoleisure.co.uk

Lundin Links has a championship golf course and beautiful sandy beaches.

4 Holiday caravans to let, sleeps 4-8.

Leisure Facilities:

3 miles from Lundin Links.

Park accommodation: 128

19585

Clayton Caravan Park

St Andrews, Fife, KY16 9YB
Tel:01334 870242 Fax:01334 8700057
Email:enquiries@clayton-caravan-park.com
Web:www.clayton-caravan-park.com

Park on slopes of River Eden.

Park accommodation: 276

8 Holiday Homes for hire, sleeps 4-6.18, Rates on application.

68973

Upper Largo, Fife

Map Ref: 2D3

Monturpie Caravan Park

Monturpie, Upper Largo, Leven, Fife, KY8 5QS
Tel:01333 360254   Fax:01333 360850
Email:enquiries@monturpie.co.uk

Caravan & camping site.

Park accommodation: **24**
Holiday Homes for hire. Rates on application.

St Monans, East Neuk of Fife

Don't wait, book now!

call: 0845 22 55 121

£4 booking fee applies to telephone bookings

VisitScotland.com

Fyvie Castle, Aberdeenshire

ABERDEEN AND GRAMPIAN HIGHLANDS
Scotland's Castle and Whisky Country

Silvery grey it may be but the 'Granite City' of Aberdeen has won more awards for its floral displays than any other city in the UK.

In 2006 it scooped a unique hat-trick, winning Scotland in Bloom for the 39th consecutive year and adding the British and International equivalents.

With 45 parks in the city and a celebrated Winter Garden at Duthie Park, Aberdeen is always in bloom and every season brings further floral flights of fancy.

A seaside city

But then, Aberdeen is a city of acute contrasts. It's an important port with links to the fishing and oil industries, it's a thriving cultural centre with a stylish selection of galleries, museums, restaurants, nightclubs and bars.

It has a busy central shopping area yet just a short distance away there's a brilliant beach complete with funfair.

The many fascinations of the Aberdeenshire coastline extend beyond the city and there are miles of golden, sandy beaches and towering cliffs to explore. All along the coast you'll find captivating harbour towns like Stonehaven, Peterhead, Fraserburgh, Banff and Macduff and quaint little places like the stunning Pennan, a former smugglers' town at the foot of a cliff.

Castles and whisky galore

Some great trails have been laid out for visitors to follow including the intriguing Castle Trail. There are over 350 castles in Aberdeen and Grampian

Highlands and they come in all shapes and sizes from fairytale castles to crumbling ruins and even royal holiday homes.

And speaking of royalty, the Deeside towns of Banchory, Ballater and Braemar have all enjoyed many decades of royal patronage, the annual highlight of which is the Braemar Gathering in September.

You may also want to take the Malt Whisky Trail which features 8 famous distilleries and a cooperage in Moray. Each tells the story of 'the water of life' in its own distinctive way and if you happen to stagger off the trail at any point, there are another 42 distilleries to discover in the Speyside area.

Alongside the whisky, there are other delights that will soon have you raising your glass – music, song and, of course, fine food. Aberdeen and Grampian Highlands is Scotland's natural larder. Beautiful Aberdeen Angus beef, sumptuous seafood, fabulous fruit and vegetables – all come fresh to the table, prepared by the finest chefs. There's even a festival to celebrate –Taste of Grampian, held annually in June at Inverurie.

So where will you find your perfect place? There's a lot of choice of high quality holiday and touring parks both inland and by the sea so whatever you require, you're sure to find it in Aberdeen and Grampian Highlands.

Dunnottar Castle, Aberdeenshire

What's On?

Burning of the Clavie, Burghead
11 January 2008
A fire festival commemorating the old New Year.

Aberdeen Jazz Festival
5 – 9 March 2008
Live jazz events with local and international artists.
www.jazzaberdeen.com

Spirit of Speyside Whisky Festival
1 – 5 May 2008
Whisky takes centre stage.
www.spiritofspeyside.com

Word Festival, Aberdeen
9 – 11 May 2008
One of the most popular literary events in Scotland.

Taste of Grampian, Inverurie
7 June 2008
A 1-day food and drink festival.
www.tasteofgrampian.co.uk

Aberdeen Highland Games
15 June 2008
A rich programme of events and competitions.
www.aberdeenhighlandgames.com

Turriff Show
3 – 4 August 2008
The largest 2-day agricultural show in Scotland.
www.turriffshow.org

Braemar Gathering
6 September 2008
The biggest Highland Games attended by the Royal Family.
www.braemargathering.org

City of Aberdeen Hogmanay Street Party
31 December 2008
Featuring a programme of live music.

Stonehaven Fireball Festival
31 December 2008
A spectacular winter fire festival to bring in the New Year.

www.aberdeen-grampian.com

DON'T MISS

1.   The railway originally came to Ballater in 1866, when Deeside Railway built its terminus here. In its heyday, many famous people – including the Tsar of Russia – used Ballater Station. Today, the building has been lovingly restored and hosts an exhibition on its amazing history.

2.   Scotland's Castle Trail winds its way between some of Scotland's finest fairytale homes and fortresses including Crathes Castle. Built in the second half of the 16th century, Crathes Castle is a splendid example of the tower house style of the time, and retains many of its original interior features. Perhaps the best reason to visit, however, is the 1½ hectare walled garden, complete with herbaceous borders and a stunning array of unusual plants. Crathes can be found 3 miles east of the town of Banchory.

3.   Found in homes and bars around the globe, Glenfiddich is the world's favourite single malt Scotch whisky. Discover the history of the Glenfiddich Distillery, owned and managed by the fifth generation of the Grant family, learn how whisky is produced and at the end of your visit enjoy a dram of Glenfiddich in the Glenfiddich Bar. A journey to the home of Glenfiddich makes you appreciate each mouthful even more.

4.   Aberdeen's beachfront is a family paradise. Take a walk along the 2 miles of soft sandy beach and discover a range of attractions on offer for all the family, as well as a mix of restaurants old and new.

5.   The Art Gallery is one of Aberdeen's most popular tourist attractions and offers a fantastic day out for art lovers and novices alike with paintings ranging from Victorian to Scottish, Impressionist to 20th century British.

6.   For the ultimate opportunity to 'get back to nature' take a wildlife tour - North 58° Sea Adventures, Troup Tours, Moray Diving and Gemini Explorer are just some of the boat operators offering the chance to spot dolphins, porpoise, seabirds and seals in stunning surroundings and if you don't have seafaring legs you can experience the fascinating wildlife of the Cairngorms National Park with WalkDeeside and Glenlivet Wildlife.

FOOD AND DRINK

www.eatscotland.com

7   The Malt Whisky Trail incorporates eight distilleries and the Speyside Cooperage. This is an excellent way to find out all about Scotland's National Drink. Indeed, two annual celebrations of whisky take place each year at the Spirit of Speyside Whisky Festival in late April/early May and the Autumn Speyside Whisky Festival in late September. Fine malts such as Glenlivet and Glenfiddich can be savoured as well as kilt-making demonstrations and tours of nearby distilleries.

8   While in the area ensure you try Cullen Skink – a thick soup made with smoked haddock. This local speciality is sure to warm you up before setting off to explore the coastal village of Cullen.

9   The Laird's Kitchen at Delgatie Castle in Turriff was voted 17th best place to have afternoon tea in Britain – a pretty little restaurant serving good food with local produce. The carrot cake is legendary and has been written about in books and magazine articles all over the world.

10   Based in Huntly is the renowned Dean's of Huntly factory, complete with a shop offering all your favourite varieties of shortbread and much more in which to indulge. Ideal for stocking up or for purchasing gifts to take home!

ACTIVITIES

11   Cullen – Logie Head – Findlater Castle – Sandend – This unspoilt coastline boasts cliffs and bays interspersed with traditional fishing villages. The walk from Cullen to the quaint village of Sandend arrives at a beautiful sandy bay – Sandside beach – and, just beyond it, Findlater Castle, an ancient ruined fortress built on a narrow promontory. The first stage of the walk is along good paths with sections of beach but the second half is less developed, so may be less manageable for some. Allow 3 hours for the full 4-mile route.

12   Where better to experience true Scottish golf than on the variety of fairways in Aberdeen and Grampian Highlands. You can choose from 25 links courses from the traditional Royal Aberdeen (6th oldest golf course in the world), Cruden Bay, Murcar and Moray Old to the amazing Cullen, Stonehaven, Royal Tarlair and Fraserburgh. There are more than 70 golf courses to get on 'par' with.

13   The sea, the lochs, the rivers. Why not hook up with a water sports company like the Surf and Watersports Club to bag a few new activities or have a go at Kite Land Boarding with Synergy Kite Sports – all the fun of surfing but without getting wet!

14   If you enjoy your snow sports nothing can quite match the thrill and breathtaking exhilaration of swooping down a snowy slope at the Glenshee Ski Centre. Or how about buggy riding in the Lecht Ski Resort (trust us, this activity has to be sampled to be believed!).

HISTORY AND HERITAGE

15 Braemar's Highland Games - The Braemar Gathering – are held on the first Saturday of September each year, and are notable for the scale and for their unique chieftain, none other than Her Majesty The Queen. Royalty is always in attendance, watching tossing the caber, Highland dancing, and piping.

16 Scottish home of the Royal Family since the mid-19th century, Balmoral Castle is a grand granite pile set amidst spectacular scenery. Seasonal opening hours allow visitors to see the ballroom – the Castle's largest room - and an audio-visual presentation provides the history of the Castle since it was purchased for Queen Victoria by Prince Albert. Visit some more of Queen Victoria's favourite spots on the Victorian Heritage Trail.

17 Designed to bring the past to life, award-winning Archaeolink Prehistory Park near the village of Insch allows you to travel 10,000 years in one day! With hands-on activities and guided tours there's plenty to interest all ages.

18 Step back in time through the last millennium on Scotland's only Castle Trail. In all 13 properties make up the trail, from fairytale Craigievar Castle to ruined Kildrummy Castle, from the distinctive turrets of Castle Fraser to the star-shaped ramparts of Corgarff Castle.

WALKS   www.visitscotland.com/walking

19 Allow around 2 hours for an enjoyable circular walk in Cairngorms National Park starting from Braemar village. Take the A93 to Glenshee for ½ mile, and then follow signs for 'Queen's Drive' and 'Lion's Face'. The track will take you through birch woodland, passing a small lochan on the left, and returns to the village.

20 The Burghead to Hopeman coastal walk will take you between two peaceful villages on the coast of Moray, past several quiet sandy beaches with views across the Moray Firth. You can start at either end, and shops, food and drink are available in either village. The path follows the track of a long disused and removed railway line. You can return by the same path or follow another alongside the shore. Allow 3 - 3½ hours for the 4 mile route.

21 Cambus O' May Forest, near Ballater, welcomes walkers of all abilities. Areas of native Scots pine and a variety of classic Scottish wildlife, such as red squirrels and crossbills, make for a pleasant stroll. There are a number of paths, some offering spectacular views of the Dee Valley below.

22 From the Bennachie Centre near Chapel of Garioch, a fabulous array of woodland walks are available through Bennachie Forest, most offering an opportunity to view sculptures and wildlife from the path. Red squirrels, roe deer and crossbills are present in good numbers, while any of Bennachie's summits offer sightings of moorland species such as grouse, pippets and buzzards.

MAP

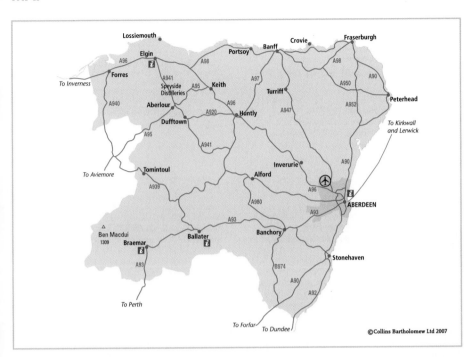

© Collins Bartholomew Ltd 2007

TOURIST INFORMATION CENTRES

Aberdeen and Grampian Highlands

Aberdeen Visitor Centre	23 Union Street, Aberdeen KY12 7DL
Ballater	The Old Royal Station, Station Square, Ballater AB35 5QB
Braemar	Unit 3, The Mews, Mar Road, Braemar AB35 5YL
Elgin	17 High Street, Elgin IV30 1EG

Make the most of your stay in Scotland and make your first stop the Tourist Information Centre wherever you go.

Knowledgeable and friendly staff can help you with information and advice; they can answer your questions, book accommodation and you can even pick up some souvenirs to take home for friends and family.

For information and ideas about exploring Scotland in advance of your trip, call our booking and information service or go to www.visitscotland.com

Call 0845 22 55 121

or if calling from outside the UK call +44 (0) 1506 832 121

From Ireland call 1800 932 510

A £4 booking fee applies to telephone bookings of accommodation.

36495 Aberdeen — Map Ref: 4G10

Lower Deeside Holiday Park

Maryculter, Aberdeen, AB12 5FX
Tel:01224 733860 Fax:01224 732490
Email:enquiries@lowerdeesideholidaypark.com
Web:www.lowerdeesideholidaypark.com

12 acres, grassy, level, hardstanding, Jan-Dec. Extra charge for awnings.

Park accommodation: **115**
56 tourers £13.00-15.00, 56 motors £13.00-15.00, 23 tents £10.00-15.00, Total Touring Pitches 68.
6 Holiday Caravans to let, sleeps 4-6, total sleeping capacity 24, £199.00-349.00 per week.

Leisure Facilities:
From Aberdeen take B9077 at Bridge of Dee r/about for 6mls. From, Stonehaven take B979 for 10mls. From Banchory take A93 for 9mls then, follow signs for Maryculter.

30557 Buckie, Banffshire — Map Ref: 4.00E+07

Strathlene Caravan Park

Portessie, Buckie, Banffshire, AB56 1SR
Tel:01542 834851 Fax:01224 696988

Touring and camping site.

Park accommodation: **62**
Holiday Homes for hire. Rates on application.

39452 Fordoun, Kincardineshire — Map Ref: 4F12

Brownmuir Caravan Park

Fordoun, Laurencekirk, Aberdeenshire, AB30 1SJ
Tel/Fax:01561 320786
Email:brownmuircaravanpark@talk21.com
Web:www.brownmuircaravanpark.co.uk

7 acres, grassy, level, sheltered, Apr-Oct. Extra charge for awnings, showers.

Park accommodation: **60**
10 tourers £11.50, 10 motors £11.50, 5 tents £8.00. Total Touring Pitches 10.
2 Holiday Caravans to let, sleeps 4-6, total sleeping capacity 10, £250.00 per week.

Leisure Facilities:
On A90 4mls N of Laurencekirk. Turn left at Fordoun Village over bridge. Park 1ml on right. Signposted.

23038 by Laurencekirk, Kincardineshire — Map Ref: 4F12

Dovecot Caravan Park

Northwater Bridge, by Laurencekirk, AB30 1QL
Tel/Fax:01674 840630
Email:adele@dovecotcaravanpark.co.uk
Web:www.dovecotcaravanpark.co.uk

6 acres, grassy, level, Apr-Oct.

Park accommodation: **70**
25 tourers £10.00-11.00, 25 motors £10.00-11.00, 25 tents £7.50-8.50, Total Touring Pitches 25.

From Laurencekirk (A90) 5mls S at Northwaterbridge, turn right to Edzell Woods. Site is 300m on left. Signposted.

24094 St Cyrus, Aberdeenshire — Map Ref: 4G12

East Bowstrips Caravan Park

St Cyrus, Nr Montrose, Aberdeenshire, DD10 0DE
Tel/Fax:01674 850328
Email:tully@bowstrips.freeserve.co.uk
Web:www.ukparks.co.uk/eastbowstrips

4 acres, grassy, hardstanding, Apr-Oct. Extra charge for showers. No charge for electric hook-up.

Park accommodation: **60**
33 tourers from £14.00, 33 motors from £14.00, 6 tents from £10.00. Total Touring Pitches 33.

From S (Montrose) on A92, enter St Cyrus, pass hotel, 1st left, 2nd right. From N (Aberdeen), enter St Cyrus and take 1st right, 2nd right. Signposted.

52951 Sandend, by Portsoy, Banffshire — Map Ref: 4F7

Sandend Caravan Park

Sandend, by Portsoy, Banffshire, AB4 2UA
Tel:01261 842660 Fax:01261 843693
Email:sandendholidays@aol.com

4 acres, grassy, level, hardstanding, Apr-Oct. Extra charge for awnings.

Park accommodation:**48**
20 tourers £12.50-15.50, 20 motors £12.50-15.50, 18 tents £9.50-12.50.
3 Holiday Caravans to let, sleeps 6, total sleeping capacity 18, £220.00-385.00 per week.

Leisure Facilities: Between Portsoy and Cullen on A98. Take turn to Sandend Caravan Park on right beside beach. Signposted.

Union Street, Aberdeen

IMPORTANT: PRICES STATED ARE ESTIMATES AND MAY BE SUBJECT TO AMENDMENTS
FOR A FULL LISTING OF QUALITY ASSURED CARAVAN AND CAMPING PARKS, PLEASE SEE DIRECTORY AT BACK OF THIS GUIDE

105

Glen Coe, Highlands

THE HIGHLANDS AND SKYE

If you're searching for tranquillity and a more balanced perspective, you'll find that life in the Highlands moves at a refreshingly relaxed pace.

Stirringly beautiful and dramatically wild, it's hard not to be moved by the rugged majesty of the mountainous north. It's the stuff of picture postcards and coffee table books and views that will be etched in your memory forever.

Unspoiled beauty

There are so many places you have to experience: the eerie silence of Glen Coe; the arctic wilderness of the Cairngorms; the deep mysteries of Loch Ness; the wild flat lands of the Flow Country; the astonishing beauty of Glen

Affric; and the golden beaches of the west coast where you can gaze out to the Atlantic and never meet a soul all day.

In this great, unspoiled, natural environment, wildlife flourishes. You'll see red squirrels and tiny goldcrests in the trees, otters chasing fish in fast flowing rivers, deer coming down from the hill to the forest edge, dolphins and whales off the coast, ospreys and eagles soaring overhead.

A natural playground

And this great natural playground is yours to share. Climbers, walkers, mountain bikers, skiers and hunters take to the hills. Surfers, sailors, canoeists and fishermen enjoy the beaches, rivers and lochs.

If it's adrenaline-filled adventure you're after you can try sports like sphereing, canyoning and white water rafting. Whatever outdoor activity you like to pursue, you'll find experienced, professional experts on hand to ensure you enjoy it to the full.

Highland hospitality

And once you've had enough exercise and fresh air, you can be assured of some fine Highland hospitality, whether you're staying near a tiny village, a pretty town, a thriving activity centre like Aviemore or the rapidly expanding city of Inverness.

In the pubs and hotels, restaurants and other venues around the community, you'll find music and laughter, perhaps a riotous ceilidh in full fling and unforgettable nights of eating and drinking into the wee small hours.

Back to your roots

Highlanders know how to enjoy life and they're always keen to welcome visitors – especially those who are tracing their Scottish roots. Every year people come to discover the traditional homeland of their clan, learn about their history and walk in their ancestors' footsteps over battlefields like Culloden where the Jacobite army made its last stand.

You could follow Bonnie Prince Charlie over the sea to Skye whether it's by boat or by bridge. You can even take a glass bottom boat trip around the island and watch the sea life below.

Wherever you decide to go, the Highlands and Skye will cast a spell on you and it will be a holiday you will remember for as long as you live.

Portree, Isle of Skye

What's On?

O'Neill Highland Open, Thurso
25 April – 1 May 2008
One of the most progressive events in competitive surfing.
www.oneilleurope.com/highlandopen

**Fèis an Eilein –
The Skye Festival, Sleat**
15 – 25 July 2008
An 11-day festival of traditional music, theatre and film.
www.feisaneilein.com

Tulloch Inverness Highland Games
19 – 20 July 2008
Clan gathering and heavyweight competition in Inverness.
www.invernesshighlandgames.com

Inverness Highland Tattoo
21 – 26 July 2008
Previewing artists from the Edinburgh International Tattoo.
www.tattooinverness.org.uk

Rock Ness, Dores, Loch Ness
7 – 8 June 2008
The only music event with its own monster.
www.rockness.co.uk

Belladrum Tartan Heart Festival, nr Inverness
8 – 9 August 2008
Open air, family-friendly traditional music festival.
www.tartanheartfestival.co.uk

UCI Mountain Bike World Cup, Fort William
7 – 8 June 2008
Voted best event on the tour 2 years running.
www.fortwilliamworldcup.co.uk

Highland Feast
26 September – 12 October 2008
A series of unique culinary and gastronomic events.
www.highlandfeast.co.uk

www.visithighlands.com

MAP

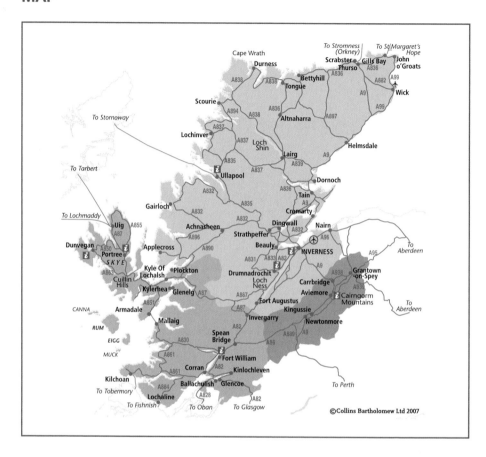

©Collins Bartholomew Ltd 2007

TOURIST INFORMATION CENTRES

Northern Highlands, Inverness, Loch Ness and Nairn

Drumnadrochit	The Car Park, Drumnadrochit, Inverness-shire IV63 6TX
Inverness	Castle Wynd, Inverness IV2 3BJ
Ullapool	6 Argyle Street, Ullapool, Ross-shire IV26 2UB

Fort William and Lochaber, Skye and Lochalsh

Dunvegan	2 Lochside, Dunvegan, Isle of Skye IV55 8WB
Fort William	15 High Street, Fort William PH33 6DH
Portree	Bayfield Road, Portree, Isle of Skye IV51 9EL

Aviemore and the Cairngorms

Aviemore	Grampian Road, Aviemore PH22 1PP

Make the most of your stay in Scotland and make your first stop the Tourist Information Centre wherever you go.

Knowledgeable and friendly staff can help you with information and advice; they can answer your questions, book accommodation and you can even pick up some souvenirs to take home for friends and family.

For information and ideas about exploring Scotland in advance of your trip, call our booking and information service or go to **www.visitscotland.com**

Call 0845 22 55 121

or if calling from outside the UK call
+44 (0) 1506 832 121

From Ireland call
1800 932 510

A £4 booking fee applies to telephone bookings of accommodation.

Loch Maree, Highlands

Northern Highlands, Inverness, Loch Ness and Nairn

Scotland's most northerly mainland territory is characterised by its mountainous, unspoiled wild places and its stunning coastline.

Within this great wilderness, there are places where nature has been tamed to dramatic effect – the celebrated Inverewe Gardens being an unmissable spot on the west coast.

Equally essential on the itinerary of any Highland visitor is Loch Ness, Britain's deepest and most mysterious freshwater expanse. Take a tour by boat and stare into its impenetrably dark waters and while you're there, don't miss the sprawling ruin of Urquhart Castle which never fails to impress.

There are many fine towns and villages to visit – Ullapool, Autlbea, Lochinver and Kinlochbervie to the west, Thurso, John O'Groats, Wick, Dornoch, Strathpeffer and Nairn on the eastern side.

You should also take some time to explore the rapidly growing city of Inverness, capital of the Highlands and a thriving, modern city with lots of attractions.

Footbridge over the River Ness, Inverness

DON'T MISS

1   Accessible by boat from Tarbet, just north of Scourie, Handa Island is home to one of Britain's
    biggest seabird colonies during spring and early summer. Under the care of the Scottish Wildlife
    Trust, there are few better – or more beautiful – sites to spot guillemots, razorbills and puffins,
    among a myriad of other species.

2   Culloden Battlefield is the site of the last major battle fought on mainland Britain in 1746.
    Bonnie Prince Charlie's Jacobite troops were defeated here by the Duke of Cumberland and the
    Hanoverian government forces. The new visitor centre – opened in 2007 – features a battle
    immersion cinema and handheld multi-lingual audio devices to bring the battle to life.

3   Not only is there a wealth of wildlife on land, but also in the waters nearby. The Beauly, Moray and
    Cromarty Firths all play host to bottlenose dolphins – the North Sea's only resident group.
    A number of boat trips departing from Nairn, Inverness or Cromarty can take you out to see them
    without disturbing their habitat – look out for members of the Dolphin Space Programme,
    accredited operators conducting cruises of high quality with low environmental impact.

4   Perhaps the most spectacularly scenic of all Scottish lochs, Loch Maree greets unsuspecting
    visitors travelling north-west on the A832 between Inverness and Gairloch. Bounded by the
    imposing masses of Beinn Eighe to the west and Slioch to the east, the loch's shores play host to
    a wealth of wildlife, as well as fragments of ancient Caledonian pinewood.

5   One of the largest castles in Scotland, the ruins of Urquhart Castle lie on the banks of Loch
    Ness, near Drumnadrochit. Blown up in 1692 to prevent Jacobite occupation, this 5-star visitor
    attraction has a fascinating interactive visitor centre which depicts the story of the castle's turbulent
    history. Explore the ruins of the castle, before visiting the on-site café where you will be rewarded
    with breathtaking views of Loch Ness.

6   At Learnie Red Rock Trails an exciting mix of short well made uphills and challenging fast
    downhill sections make for a great day's mountain biking on the Black Isle with fantastic views of
    the Moray Firth. Situated in woodland on the A832 between Rosemarkie and Cromarty this
    attraction will fill your adrenaline needs.

FOOD AND DRINK

www.eatscotland.com

7   In the attractive fishing settlement of Achiltibuie, the Summer Isles Hotel boasts an
    astounding menu and even better views. Enjoy the local seafood while the sun sets over its
    namesake islands. Five miles north, the Smokehouse allows you to see delicious fish being cured
    and gives you the chance to purchase it afterwards.

8   Highland Feast, an annual food and drink festival held in late September/early October, is a
    celebration of the fantastic produce and culinary skills present in the local area and beyond.

9   Fresh, local ingredients are combined to make the Falls of Shin Visitor Centre the
    ultimate place to stop for lunch. See salmon leap on the magnificent waterfall as you tuck in.
    There is also a children's playground so you can fill up while the kids are kept entertained.

10 On the A82 near Inverness, at Moniack Castle Wineries, see how a selection of 9 wines
    and liqueurs and 22 marmalades, preserves and sauces are made from the best of natural
    Highland ingredients. Tour the fermenting room, filtering processes, bottling and labelling, then
    pass through the cellars to the kitchen and watch the cooking of the preserves and sauces.

GOLF

www.visitscotland.com/golf

11 Gairloch Golf Course is superbly situated above a sandy bay beside the road into
    Gairloch. This 9-hole links course is one of the Highland's best kept secrets. Take your time
    soaking up the views towards Skye. Arrange tee times in advance to guarantee a round.

12 Durness Golf Course, surrounded by stunning coastal scenery, is notorious for its 9th hole,
    which requires players to clear the Atlantic Ocean! Check with the secretary in advance to ensure
    a round is possible.

13 Considered one of the finest links courses in the world, Royal Dornoch Golf Course is
    situated on public land in its namesake royal burgh, 45 miles north of Inverness. Play on the course
    about which Tom Watson famously remarked 'the most fun I've ever had on a golf course'.

14 A traditional Scottish links course, Brora Golf Course offers a challenge for all abilities.
    Situated on the northeast coast, 20 minutes drive from Dornoch, this 18-hole favourite is perfect
    for the discerning golfer looking to experience a course steeped in tradition.

OUTSTANDING VIEWS

15 A classic view of Loch Ness is to be savoured from the beach at the village of Dores, at the quieter side of the Loch to the south. Look out for Nessie, or at the very least, the resident Nessie spotter!

16 Round the bay from Lochinver, a minor road allows fantastic views back towards the community and the incredible sugar loaf of Suilven rising up in the background.

17 Near John o'Groats see a dramatic coastline where thousands of seabirds nest in vast colonies. A walk across the clifftop fields will reward you with a stunning view south to Thirle Door and the Stacks of Duncansby. The first is a rocky arch, the second a group of large jagged sea stacks. This is a spot you will want to savour, with a view that varies as you move along the clifftop path and bring into play different alignments of the stacks and arch.

18 The Corrieshalloch Gorge National Nature Reserve, south-east of Ullapool, comprises a box canyon dropping 200ft to the river below. Adding to the drama are the spectacular Falls of Measach, best seen from the viewing platform to the north.

WALKS   www.visitscotland.com/walking

19 Reelig Glen is a short walk through spectacular old conifer and broad-leaved trees on easy paths with short gentle gradients, making it a suitable walk for almost anyone. Approximately 10 minutes from Inverness, take the A862 west towards Beauly and after 8 miles, turn left onto the minor road signposted to Reelig and Moniack and continue for 1 mile – follow the Forestry Commission sign and look out for one of Britain's tallest trees named Dughall Mor.

20 Gentle walking or cycling awaits through an extensive network of formal and informal trails at Culbin Forest between Nairn and Forres. Forest trails, guided walks and a badger hide are among the many attractions of this forest, which hosts a variety of plant, animal and bird life.

21 Take the minor B869 road to Storr lighthouse, from which a 3-hour circular walk leads to a spectacular rock-stack – the Old Man of Stoer - surrounded by jaw-dropping cliff scenery. The path is clear throughout, and offers views to the Assynt mountains in the south, and to Lewis and Harris many miles to the west.

22 The Caithness and Sutherland Walking Festival, held in May, consists of themed walks led by local guides. These interesting walks explore archaeology, history and wildlife and are a great way to learn more about the surrounding area.

68940

30 Mellon Charles

Aultbea, by Achnasheen, Ross-shire, IV22 2JN
Tel:01445 731499
Email:aultbeacaravans@hotmail.com

Jan-Dec.

Park accommodation: 1 ⬚⬚

£130.00-190.00 per week.

51469

Scottish TOURIST BOARD ★★★★ TOURING PARK

Reraig Caravan Site

Balmacara, Kyle of Lochalsh, Ross-shire, IV40 8DH
Tel:01599 566215
Email:warden@reraig.com
Web:www.reraig.com

2 acres, mixed, May-Sep, Extra charge for electricity, awnings, showers.

Park accommodation:40 ⬚⬚⬚

Total Touring Pitches 45. Prices on application or see, website.

On A87 5½ mls W of Eilean Donan Castle, Dornie. 4 mls E of Skye Bridge. Signposted.

22963

Scottish TOURIST BOARD ★★★★ HOLIDAY PARK
Thistle

Dornoch Caravan Park

The Links, River Street, Dornoch, Sutherland, IV25 3LX
Tel/Fax:01862 810423
Email:info@dornochcaravans.co.uk
Web:www.dornochcaravans.co.uk

25 acres, grassy, Apr-Oct 23rd. Extra charge for electricity, awnings.

Park accommodation: 200 ⬚⬚⬚⬚

120 tourers £9.50-12.50, 120 motors £9.50-12.50, 120 tents £9.00-11.00, Total Touring Pitches 120.

6 Holiday Caravans to let, sleeps 4-6, total sleeping capacity 36, £140.00-340.00 per week.

Leisure Facilities: ●❄

6 mls N of Tain turn right off A9 to Dornoch. 2mls on at bottom of main square turn right for 400 yds.

31889

Scottish TOURIST BOARD ★★★ TOURING PARK

Inver Caravan Park

Houstry Road, Dunbeath, Caithness, KW6 6EH
Tel:01593 731441   Fax:01593 731477
Email:rhonagwilliam@yahoo.co.uk
Web:www.inver-caravan-park.co.uk

1 acre of grass, 3 hard standings, free showers.

Park accommodation: 15 ⬚⬚⬚

All caravans, motor-homes, tents, trailer-tents, cars and vans.

Holiday Caravan for hire, sleeps up to 6, from £27.00-47.00 per night, £160.00-280.00 per week.

18007

Scottish TOURIST BOARD ★★★★ CAMPING PARK

Badrallach DB&B, Bothy, Cottage & Camp Site

Croft No 9, Badrallach, Dundonnell, Ross-shire
IV23 2QP
Tel:01854 633281
Email:mail@badrallach.com
Web:www.badrallach.com

1 acres, grassy, level, Jan-Dec.

3 tourers £10.00, 3 motors £10.00, 12 tents £10.00. Total Touring Pitches 15.

1 Holiday Cottage to let, sleeps 4, £190.00-350.00 per week.
1 Bothy to let, sleeps 12, £60.00 per night sole use.

Leisure Facilities: ●❄

Take single track road off A832 1 mile E of hotel. Signposted.

Park accommodation: 19 ⬚⬚⬚

Sands Holiday Centre

Gairloch, Ross-shire, IV21 2DL
Tel:01445 712152 Fax:01445 712518
Email:litsands@aol.com
Web:www.sandsholidaycentre.co.uk

55 acres, grassy, sandy, Easter-mid Oct. Extra charge for electricity, awnings.

Park accommodation: **250**
Total Touring Pitches 200. From £8.50-12.50 based on, caravan, car and 2 people.
5 Holiday Caravans to let, sleeps 6, total sleeping capacity 30, £325.00-485.00 per week.

Follow the A832 to Gairloch. Take B8021 to Melvaig. 4 mls along to Holiday Centre. Signposted.

Auchnahillin Caravan & Camping Park

Daviot East, Inverness-shire, IV2 5XQ
Tel:01463 772286
Email:info@auchnahillin.co.uk
Web:www.auchnahillin.co.uk

10 acres, family-run park.

Park accommodation: **100**
45 pitches for tourers, 30 tents.
10 static caravan holiday homes and one chalet for hire.

John O'Groats Caravan Site

John O'Groats, Caithness, KW1 4YR
Tel:01955 611329/744
Email:info@johnogroatscampsite.co.uk
Web:www.johnogroatscampsite.co.uk

4 acres, grassy, level, hardstanding, Apr-Sep. Extra charge for electricity, awnings, showers.

Park accommodation: **90**
90 tourers £12.00, 90 motors £12.00, 90 car/tents £10.00. Total Touring Pitches 90.
Follow A9. Join A99 at Latherton Jnct. Continue to end of road at John O'Groats.

Halladale Inn Caravan Park

Melvich, Sutherland, KW14 7YJ
Tel/Fax:01641 531282
Email:mazfling@tinyworld.co.uk
Web:www.halladaleinn.co.uk

¼ acre, grassy, hardstanding, Apr-Oct. Extra charge for electricity, awnings.

Park accommodation: **14**
6 tourers £10.00, 6 motors £10.00, 8 tents £5.00 per person. Total Touring Pitches 14.
17 miles W of Thurso along A836. Signposted.

Elgol, Loch Scavaig, Isle of Skye

Fort William, Lochaber, Skye and Lochalsh

Fort William is often referred to as the 'Outdoor Capital of the UK'. It has been host to the Mountain Biking World Championships, it's next door to Ben Nevis, Scotland's highest mountain, and the surrounding area provides a bewildering range of opportunities to enjoy the outdoors.

The local scenery is quite stunning. From the towering beauty of Glen Coe to the breathtaking views across Loch Duich from Castle Stalker to the wild isolation of Ardnamurchan Point, there are hundreds of amazing places to visit.

Why not take in some of the finest coastal and hill scenery on what is considered one of the Great Railway Journeys of the World. Travel the length of the legendary Road to the Isles on the Jacobite Steam Train from Fort William to Mallaig. Take in such sites as the Caledonian Canal, the Glenfinnan Viaduct and the glorious coastline of Arisaig and Morar, and when you reach Mallaig you'll be able to see the jagged peaks of the Cuillin Mountains on the Isle of Skye.

The turbulent history and majestic scenery of Skye and Lochalsh make the area one of Scotland's most romantic destinations. From the delightfully situated Eilean Donan Castle and the picture-postcard village of Plockton to the soaring craggy heights of the Cuillin and the eerie pinnacles of the Trotternish, the area is sure to leave an imprint on your heart.

DON'T MISS

1   One of the most picturesque – and most photographed – castles in Scotland, Eilean Donan Castle, sits on an island in Loch Duich, beside the tiny village of Dornie. Stroll across the causeway that links it to the shore and explore it for yourself. For a panoramic view, follow the path from the village which leads up to the Carr Brae viewpoint.

2   Take a boat trip from Elgol to isolated and inspiring Loch Coruisk. You will get up close to Britain's most dramatic landscapes, while your local guide will make sure you don't miss out on seeing the local wildlife – including the famous seal colony on the banks of the Loch.

3   Accessible only by boat from Mallaig or via a very long walk from Kinlochhourn, Knoydart is recognised as the remotest part of mainland Britain and is perfect for the adventurous. One of the best hiking spots in the country, there are also options for wildlife watching, canoeing and fishing, amongst other activities organised by operators in the area. The scenery is outstanding and will leave a lasting impression.

4   Familiar to fans of the film Local Hero, and every bit as stunning in reality, Camusdarach Beach is one of a string of exquisite beaches along the shoreline between Arisaig and Morar. While away a few hours picnicking with the breathtaking backdrop of the Small Isles rising sheer out of the sea in front of you. For an alternative, try the Silver Sands of Morar to the north.

5   To travel the whole length of the legendary Road to the Isles, hop aboard the Jacobite Steam Train. This steam engine runs between Fort William and Mallaig throughout the summer months and takes in some truly impressive sites such as Neptune's Staircase, the Glenfinnan Viaduct and the glorious coastline of Arisaig and Morar. Regarded as one of the Great Railway Journeys of the World, this is a must while in the area, especially for Harry Potter fans who will recognise it from the movies.

6   The biggest indoor ice climbing facility in the world, The Ice Factor, is situated in a former aluminium works in Kinlochleven. With rock climbing walls, a gym, sauna, and plunge pool, this is a great day out for the activity enthusiast or indeed, the whole family. As the National Centre for Indoor Ice Climbing, experts can try out new techniques whilst novices can get to grips with the basics in a safe and secure environment.

FOOD AND DRINK
www.eatscotland.com

7   The Three Chimneys restaurant is known far and wide as one of the most romantic eateries in the land. The candlelit crofter's cottage on the shores of Loch Dunvegan, voted 28th in Restaurant Magazine's 'definitive list' of the World's Top 50 Restaurants, is an idyllic setting for a proposal, a honeymoon or any special occasion. Book ahead to ensure your table.

8   Mallaig is the place to go if you're looking for fresh, locally-caught seafood in the area. The Cabin has a good value menu, and does a mean fish and chips.

9   Crannog at the Waterfront in Fort William serves the very best in seafood. Be sure to give their speciality a try – the langoustine fresh from Loch Linnhe!

10 For an AA rosette dinner, seek out Russell's Restaurant, Smiddy House in Spean Bridge. Innovation and flair are deftly applied to a fine range of local produce.

WALKS
www.visitscotland.com/walking

11 Glen Finnan - From the Glenfinnan Visitor Centre car park, follow the Mallaig road across a bridge and then look out for a sign pointing towards Glenfinnan Lodge. From here continue up the Glen where kids will be impressed by the famous viaduct, featured in the Harry Potter films. An easy 5½-mile route, taking in most of this scenic glen, can be completed in roughly 2 hours.

12 Morar to Loch Morar and Mallaig - This is a walk you can enjoy without the hassle of taking the car. The starting and finishing points are both adjacent to train stations, so check out www.firstscotrail.com to ensure you're onboard! Set off from Morar station and walk south, taking a left turn onto the minor road along Loch Morar's north shore. Keep a look out for Nessie's cousin 'Morag' who supposedly occupies this loch. Continue along, as the road becomes a path, before arriving in Tarbet. Here, a boat departs daily at 3.30 pm throughout the summer to take you back via Loch Nevis to the connecting train at Mallaig. Allow 6 hours for the walk.

13 Glen Coe is one of the most popular hiking destinations in Scotland with the likes of Allt Coire for more experienced hikers and, for the less experienced walker, places like the Lost Valley to seek out. From the car parks on the A82, the path takes you across the bridge over the River Coe towards the triple buttresses known as the Three Sisters. Turn right after the bridge and follow the trail upwards. After a couple of miles you'll reach the false summit marking the edge of the hidden basin where the MacDonald clan used to hide their cattle in times of attack.

14 For a longer more challenging walk, drive 6 miles north from Portree on the Isle of Skye, where you will find a car park. A path leads through woodland onto a steep climb to an area of geological formations. There are then a number of paths that can be followed to the base of the Old Man of Storr. Along the way you can enjoy good views across the Sound of Raasay. This walk should take in excess of 3 hours.

OUTSTANDING VIEWS

15   Quite apart from the rock formations, it is well worth the hike to Storr for the views of the western seaboard. The mountains and sea lochs of Wester Ross are perhaps more reminiscent of Norway than Scotland.

16   From Rannoch Moor on the A82, the twin peaks of Buachaille Etive Mor and Buachaille Etive Beag spectacularly mark the entrance to Glen Coe. Appearing like steep-sided pyramids they stand sentinel on the moor, offering a glimpse of the wild landscape just around the corner.

17   There are many classic views of the Cuillin Ridge. However, for sheer drama, few views in all of Scotland compare with the sight of Sgurr Nan Gillean rearing up behind Sligachan Bridge, or the full mountain range rising almost sheer from Loch Scavaig, opposite the tiny village of Elgol, west of Broadford.

18   To see the Five Sisters of Kintail from Ratagan Pass, take the Glenelg road from Shiel Bridge on the A87. As you rise up towards Mam Ratagan, about a mile along, take a look back over Loch Duich, framed by the majestic peaks of Kintail. Simply stunning.

HERITAGE

19   Dunvegan Castle, the stronghold of the MacLeod chiefs for nearly 800 years, remains their home today. Although it still has the atmosphere of a family home it is open to the public so that you can share in the unique possessions of beauty and interest. Highland cattle roam around the estate, making you feel that you've well and truly reached the Scottish Highlands!

20   Kilmuir, home of the Skye Museum of Island Life, comprises a group of seven thatched-roof cottages depicting past life on Skye, including items used by Bonnie Prince Charlie and Flora MacDonald.

21   For a full interpretation of this amazing setting, head to the Glencoe Visitor Centre on the A82, 17 miles south of Fort William. Particularly eco-friendly, this centre provides a great viewing platform, as well as an interactive exhibit for kids of all ages where you can find out how it feels to climb on ice!

22   The West Highland Museum is to be found in Fort William and houses a collection of artefacts that dates from Mesolithic times to the modern day. All elements of society are included, from crofters to soldiers and princes to clergy.

28679 | Arisaig, Inverness-shire | Map Ref: 3F11

Gorten Sands Caravan Site

Gorten Farm, Arisaig, Inverness-shire, PH39 4NS
Tel:01687 450283

6 acres, mixed, Open May-Sep. Extra charge for electricity, awnings, showers.

Park accommodation: **45**

45 tourers £12.50, 45 motors £10.50-12.50. Total Touring Pitches 45.

A830 Fort William-Mallaig road. Turn left signposted 'Back of Keppoch', 1 ml to road end over cattle grid. Signposted.

34141 | Arisaig, Inverness-shire | Map Ref: 3F11

Kinloid Cottages & Caravans

Kinloid, Arisaig, PH39 4NS
Tel:01687 450366 Fax:01687 450611
Email:gillies_alastair@yahoo.co.uk
Web:www.kinloid-arisaig.co.uk

Open Apr-Oct.

4 Holiday Caravans to let, sleeps 4-6, total sleeping capacity 30, £190.00-290.00 per week.

Pass Arisaig village church on left. Turn right for Kinloid, 3rd house on right. Signposted.

Park accommodation: **6**

27935 | Fort William, Inverness-shire | Map Ref: 3H12

Glen Nevis Holiday Caravans

Glen Nevis, Fort William, PH33 6SX
Tel:01397 702191 Fax:01397 703904
Email:holidays@glen-nevis.co.uk
Web:www.glen-nevis.co.uk

Mixed, Mar-Oct. See display advert on page 122.

Park accommodation: **280**

28 Holiday Caravans to let, sleeps 2-6,, total sleeping capacity, £315.00-540 per week.

On A82 (Glasgow-Inverness) proceed to mini r/about at northern outskirts, of Fort William. Exit S for Glen Nevis. Park 2 mls on right. Signposted.

35623 | Fort William, Inverness-shire | Map Ref: 3H12

Linnhe Lochside Holidays

Corpach, Fort William, Inverness-shire, PH33 7NL
Tel:01397 772376 Fax:01397 772007
Email:relax@linnhe-lochside-holidays.co.uk
Web:www.linnhe-lochside-holidays.co.uk

20 acres, level, sheltered, hardstanding, Mar-Oct. Extra charge for awnings. See display advert on page 123.

Park accommodation: **190**

65 tourers £14.50-16.50, 65 motors £14.50-16.50, 20 tents £11.00-13.00. Total Touring Pitches 85.

60 Holiday Caravans to let, sleeps 2-8, total sleeping capacity 270, £195.00-480.00 per week.

Leisure Facilities:

On A830, 1 ml W of Corpach village. 5 mls from Fort William, Signposted.

51261 | Glencoe, Argyll | Map Ref: 1F1

Red Squirrel Camp Site

Leacantuim Farm, Glencoe, Argyll, PA49 4HX
Tel:01855 811256
Email:squirrels@amserve.net
Web:www.redsquirrelcampsite.com

Jan-Dec, Extra charge for showers, hairdryers. Awnings over 6mtr and tents extra, gazebo's £6.00 per night.

Park accommodation: **200**

Tents £7.00 per person nightly. Kids under 12yrs 50p. No need to book other than holiday weekends.

A82 Glencoe village. Up main street, over hump bridge and on 1½ mls. Loop road off A82. Look for squirrel signs.

71207   Glencoe, Argyll   Map Ref: 1F1

Invercoe Caravan Camping Park

Glencoe, Argyll, PH49 4HP
Tel:01855 811210
Email:holidays@invercoe.co.uk
Web:www.invercoe.co.uk

5 acres, grassy, level, hardstanding, Jan-Dec,, Extra charge for awnings.

60 tourers £15.00-17.00, 60 motors £15.00-17.00, 60 tents £12.00-14.00, Total Touring Pitches 60.

4 Holiday Caravans to let, sleeps 2-4, total sleeping capacity 20, £280.00-450.00 per week.

¼ ml off A82 at Glencoe Hotel onto B863 rd to Lochleven. Park is first turn left. Signposted.

Park accommodation: **60**

16854   Roy Bridge, Inverness-shire   Map Ref: 3H12

Bunroy Camping and Caravaning Site

Roy Bridge, Inverness-shire, PH31 4AG
Tel:01397 712332 Fax:01397 712045
Email:info@bunroycamping.co.uk
Web:www.bunroycamping.co.uk

Surrounded by woodland with river border and mountain views. A great base for walking or touring with stunning scenery and many activities to choose from nearby.

3 acres, mixed, Mar-Oct.

25 tourers £14.00-15.00, 25 motors £14.00-15.00, 25 tents £10.00-11.00. Total Touring Pitches 25.

From A86 in Roy Bridge, turn opposite Stronlossit Inn, keep straight lane to end. Signposted.

Park accommodation: **25**

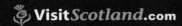

Glen Nevis® Caravan and Camping Park

AA Campsite of the Year for Scotland 2006

Popular Caravan and Camping Park set amidst beautiful Highland scenery at the foot of Ben Nevis

- Clean and Modern Facilities
- Separate Caravan and Tent areas
- Fully Serviced Caravan Pitches
- Restaurant and Bar
- Well-stocked Shop
- Self-Catering Accommodation

Set apart from our Caravan and Camping Park we have a range of high quality self-catering accommodation to let.

- From £260 per week
- Caravans, Cottages, Lodges
- 5* and 3* STB Graded
- Salmon Fishing Available
- Restaurant and Bar
- Linen and Towels Provided

Tel: 01397 702 191 - www.glen-nevis.co.uk
Glen Nevis, Fort William, PH33 6SX

Almost a botanical garden, Linnhe is recognised as one of the best and most beautful Lochside parks in Britain. Magnificent gardens contrast with the wild, dramatic scenery of Loch Eil and the

 mountains beyond. Superb amenities, launderette, shop & bakery, and free fishing on private shoreline with its own jetty all help give Linnhe its Five Star grading. Linnhe Lochside Holidays is ideally situated for

day trips with Oban, Skye, Mull, Inverness and the Cairngorms all within easy driving distance.

◇ **Holiday Caravans from £240 per week**
◇ **Touring pitches from £16 per night**
◇ **Tent pitches from £12 per night**
◇ **Pets welcome**
◇ **Tourer playground, pet exercise area**
◇ **Motorhome waste and water facilities**
◇ **Recycling on park**
◇ **Colour brochure sent with pleasure.**

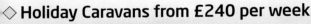

www.linnhe-lochside-holidays.co.uk/brochure
Tel: 01397 772 376 to check availability

IMPORTANT: PRICES STATED ARE ESTIMATES AND MAY BE SUBJECT TO AMENDMENTS
FOR A FULL LISTING OF QUALITY ASSURED CARAVAN AND CAMPING PARKS, PLEASE SEE DIRECTORY AT BACK OF THIS GUIDE

123

Loch Linnhe, near Fort William

A sailing lesson on Loch Morlich with a view to the Cairngorms

Aviemore and the Cairngorms

If you love the outdoor life, you'll be impressed by the many activities on offer around Aviemore and the Cairngorms.

For watersports including canoeing, sailing and windsurfing, head for Loch Insh or Loch Morlich. Mountaineers will find the Cairngorm range is always a challenge while more leisurely walkers can ramble to their heart's content in places like Glenmore Forest Park, Rothiemurchus Estate, Inshriach Forest, Craigellachie National Nature Reserve, Glenlivet Estate and many other wonderful places. Pop in to a local Tourist Information Centre for advice.

And while you're travelling round you'll see so much wildlife, crossbills, crested tits, capercaillie, red squirrels and pine martens in the forests, hare, ptarmigan, dotterel and snow buntings on the peaks.

You can cycle too – try Laggan Wolftrax for top mountain biking action and you can ski in the winter at CairnGorm Mountain and The Lecht.

There are also lots of opportunities for golfing – and fishing, of course. You can even take a steam train trip from Aviemore to Boat of Garten and Broomhill or you can scale mighty Cairn Gorm on the funicular railway.

Pony trekking near Aviemore

DON'T MISS

1   The **Cairngorms National Park** offers many events and activities throughout the year which are suitable for all ages and abilities. Visitor centres and ranger bases have leaflets, guides and trail maps to help you make the most of your time in the Park, and Tourist Information Centres throughout the area will be able to provide you with local information on events, attractions and activities.

2   At the heart of the beautiful Cairngorms National Park is the **CairnGorm Mountain Railway**. It takes eight minutes from bottom to top, where an interactive exhibition tells the history and ecology of the surrounding area and you can see some stunning panoramic views of the National Park. Have a bite to eat and take in the view stretching from the Cairngorm plateau to the Monadhliath Mountains and beyond.

3   Spend the day at **Landmark Forest Heritage Park** in Carrbridge and follow the Tree Top Trails, the Red Squirrel Trail or the Timber Trails complete with fire tower! See a steam powered sawmill and explore Microworld (a hands-on exhibition). Cap it all off with a ride on the spectacular Wildwater Coaster. There's plenty to keep everyone – young and old – amused.

4   Step back in time to the **Highland Folk Museum** with sites in Kingussie and Newtonmore, where you can experience over 400 years of Highland life. Re-constructions of an 18th century Highland township and 20th century working croft can be seen at Newtonmore. Both locations have programmes of live demonstrations and activities where you can see traditional skills and crafts in action.

5   Take to the water at **Loch Morlich** or **Loch Insh** and try your hand at sailing, canoeing, windsurfing or rowing in picturesque surroundings. Both centres offer a range of hire options from ½ hour sessions to full days, or if you're complete beginners, try the 1½ -2 hour introductory courses.

6   Drive amongst wolves, bison and Highland cattle roaming free at the **Highland Wildlife Park** in Kincraig. Featuring a number of different habitats, you can see the amazing variety of animals found in present day Scotland and also many of the animals that inhabited our countryside in years gone by. Each day, at breakfast time – that's 10am for the animals at the park – your car can follow the patrol vehicle as the warden hands out food.

FOOD AND DRINK   www.eatscotland.com

7   At **The Old Bridge Inn**, on the outskirts of Aviemore, the staff are friendly and the service is excellent. A selection of meat, game and fish awaits and all dishes are cooked simply and with flair. The dining room adjacent to the bar area allows more formal and romantic dining with its open fire, and the puddings are all home-made and vary from day to day.

8   At the Speyside Heather Centre, near Dulnain Bridge, **The Clootie Dumpling** restaurant has established a reputation for delicious hot meals and home baking. It offers the perfect opportunity to sample its namesake. This traditional and versatile pudding can be enjoyed in a variety of different ways from sweet to savoury. The recipe has a mixture of spices, carrots, apple, raisins and more, all mixed together in a 'cloot' (muslin cloth), steamed for hours and served with accompaniments.

9   Dine at **Craggan Mill** in the picturesque water mill near Grantown-on-Spey. Fine dining in a relaxed environment offers you the choice of bistro lunch or à la carte evening meal – all prepared from local, seasonal produce. Local artists exhibit paintings for view and sale within the restaurant and gallery.

10   Stylish and creative food at **The Boat Hotel** in Boat of Garten is presented in an intimate and restful atmosphere. Seasonal menus and a hand-picked wine list ensure you experience classic Scottish fayre.

ACTIVITIES

11   Take a step back in time and travel by steam engine. The **Strathspey Railway** runs from Aviemore to Broomhill (also known as Glenbogle from the TV series Monarch of the Glen) and affords beautiful views of the Cairngorms from the carriage window. To make the trip really special, you can even have afternoon tea on board.

12   **Insh Marshes Bird Reserve** is a birdwatching paradise! Around half of all British Goldeneyes nest at Inch Marshes in spring. You're also likely to see lapwings, redshanks and curlews, as well as oystercatchers, snipe and wigeon. In winter, the marshes host flocks of whooper swans and greylag geese. Roe deer, wildcats, otters and foxes may all be seen along the edges of the marshes.

13   Just outside Aviemore and Kincraig is **Alvie Stables**, a great place to try pony trekking. With hundreds of acres of National Park to ride through, the scenery will keep you engrossed.

14   The **Laggan WolfTrax** centre near Newtonmore, offers purpose built mountain bike trails with a range of options from the fun park to the double black route! Base Camp MTB provides bike hire so you don't even have to take your own, and also hires out safety equipment like knee pads to prevent any unwanted injuries! Suitable from 10 years old.

WALKS

www.visitscotland.com/walking

15 Follow the circular walk in upper Glen Feshie (from Kincraig on the B970) to the ruins of the bothy where Landseer did preliminary sketches for his Monarch of the Glen painting. The views over the Spey Valley are stunning and you may even spot red deer. The old bridge and adjacent falls offer the perfect picnic spot in fine weather.

16 Glenmore Forest Park has a range of walks from all-ability trails suitable for pushchairs, to longer walks through beautiful woodland which open out to give fantastic views of the Cairngorm Mountains. The visitor centre provides an audio-visual presentation plus café, toilets and shop.

17 There are a variety of waymarked trails throughout the Rothiemurchus Estate, with maps available from the visitor centre. The Estate is teeming with Highland wildlife, including the red squirrel and the rare capercaillie, with guided tours available courtesy of Scottish Natural Heritage. Free tours on Tuesdays.

18 The 5½ mile walk from Aviemore to Boat of Garten incorporates part of the Speyside Way. The walk goes through heather moors and woodland and gives great views of the Cairngorm Mountains. If you're too tired to walk back, then take the return trip on the Strathspey Steam Railway.

ATTRACTIONS

19 The Cairngorm Reindeer Centre is home to the only reindeer herd in the country and you can encounter the animals grazing in their natural environment. During the guided visits you can wander freely among the reindeer, stroking and feeding them. These friendly deer are a delight to all ages and, if you feel especially fond of one, you might be able to adopt it!

21 The Macdonald Aviemore Highland Resort, located in the heart of the town, offers guests accommodation and activity packages throughout the summer. For non-guests access to the fantastic swimming pool, toddlers' pool, wave machine and giant flume can be a great way to spend a rainy day.

22 Join in the working day of a Highland shepherd and his dogs at Working Sheepdogs, Leault Farm, Kincraig. As well as seeing sheepdog demonstrations you can help to shear a sheep and bottle feed the orphaned lambs or make new friends with the farm's collie puppies.

28874

Grantown-on-Spey, Moray   Map Ref: 4C9

Grantown on Spey Caravan Park

Seafield Avenue, Grantown on Spey, Morayshire,
PH26 3JQ
Tel:01479 872474   Fax:01479 873696

Landscaped park with plots for tourers or camping.,
Caravan Club site open to members and non-members.

Park accommodation: **154**

Holiday Homes for hire and/or sale.

Loch Morlich, Aviemore

IMPORTANT: PRICES STATED ARE ESTIMATES AND MAY BE SUBJECT TO AMENDMENTS
FOR A FULL LISTING OF QUALITY ASSURED CARAVAN AND CAMPING PARKS, PLEASE SEE DIRECTORY AT BACK OF THIS GUIDE

129

Stornoway, Isle of Lewis, Outer Hebrides

THE OUTER ISLANDS
Outer Hebrides, Orkney, Shetland

There's something very special about island holidays and Scotland has so many wonderful islands to explore.

On an island holiday, you can leave all the stresses and strains of mainland life far behind. You don't have to settle for just one destination either – try a bit of island hopping, there's a lot of choice.

A different pace

At Scotland's western edge, the Outer Hebrides look out to the Atlantic swell and life moves at a relaxed pace. In this last Gaelic stronghold, a warm welcome awaits.

You can get there by ferry from Oban or Uig on Skye or by plane. Fly to Barra and you'll land on the beach at low tide!

Lewis is the largest of the Outer Hebrides with a busy town at Stornoway and historical sites like the standing stones at Calanais stretching back over 3,000 years. It's distinctly different from the more mountainous Harris. Don't forget to visit the traditional weavers making the wonderful Harris Tweed.

The Uists, Benbecula, Eriskay and Barra are all well worth a visit too and each has its own attractions.

Life at the crossroads

Island life can also be experienced in Scotland's two great northern archipelagos. Some 70 islands make up Orkney with 17 inhabited. Shetland, at the crossroads where the Atlantic meets the North Sea, has over 100 islands and is home to around 22,000 people and well over a million seabirds.

In Orkney, you can see the oldest houses in northern Europe at Papa Westray, dating back to 3800 BC.

The influence of the Vikings is everywhere. Orcadians spoke Old Norse until the mid 1700s and the ancient Viking Parliament used to meet at Scalloway in Shetland.

These parts enjoy long summer days and at midsummer it never really gets dark. You can even play midnight golf in the 'Simmer Dim'.

In winter, the nights are long but the islanders have perfected the art of indoor life. Musicians fill the bars and community halls and there always seems to be something to celebrate.

Two great unmissable events are the winter fire festival of Up Helly Aa at Lerwick and the Ba' in Kirkwall, Orkney where up to 400 players take to the streets for a great rough and tumble that is somewhere between football, rugby and all-out war.

Have a wild time

Orkney and Shetland are a joy for wildlife watchers. There are millions of birds to observe as well as otters, seals, dolphins and whales. Being surrounded by sea, angling, yachting, sea kayaking, cruising and diving are readily available.

Wherever you decide to experience island life, remember that island holidays are a popular choice and while there is a reasonable number of island based camping and caravan sites, it does make sense to book well in advance.

Eshaness, Shetland

What's On?

Up Helly Aa, Shetland
29 January 2008
In Lerwick they burn a Viking galley at this fire festival.

Orkney Jazz Weekend
25 – 27 April 2008
A weekend of jazz with local and visiting performers.
www.stromnesshotel.com

Shetland Folk Festival
1 – 4 May 2008
Every year sees another eclectic line-up.
www.shetlandfolkfestival.com

Orkney Folk Festival
22 – 25 May 2008
The best in modern and traditional folk music.
www.orkneyfolkfestival.com

Johnsmas Foy, Shetland
19 – 29 June 2008
The Festival of the Sea.
www.johnsmasfoy.co.uk

St Magnus Festival, Orkney
20 – 25 June 2008
Midsummer celebration of the Arts.
www.stmagnusfestival.com

Lewis Golf Week, Stornoway
5 – 12 July 2008
A week of golf at Stornoway Golf Club.

Taransay Fiddle Week
14 – 18 July 2008
Learn new skills from leading fiddlers.

Hebridean Celtic Festival
16 – 19 July 2008
Biggest homecoming party of the year.
www.hebceltfest.com

Harris Arts Festival
4 – 9 August 2008
Celebrate arts and crafts on the island.

Orkney International Science Festival
4 – 10 September 2008
A kaleidoscopic mix of insights, ideas and activities.
www.oisf.org

Accordion and Fiddle Festival, Shetland
9 -13 October 2008
Musicians from all over the world perform.

www.visithebrides.com
www.visitorkney.com
www.visitshetland.com

All dates correct at time of publication. Please check before booking. VisitScotland cannot be held responsible for any inaccuracies.

131

DON'T MISS

1   The peace and tranquillity found here, blended with the vibrant nature of the people and their language, has been a true inspiration to many, demonstrated in the islands' crafts, music and culture. Arts venues such as An Lanntair in Stornoway and Taigh Chearsabhagh in Uist often attract internationally renowned performers and artists.

2   The 5,000 year old Calanais Standing Stones on the west side of Lewis are one of the most famous landmarks in the Outer Hebrides. These mystical stones are unique in their cross-shaped layout which has caused endless fascinating debate.

3   Seallam! Visitor Centre in Northton at the southern end of Harris presents a variety of fascinating exhibitions on the history and natural environment of the Hebrides. There is also a tea and coffee bar and a small craft shop.

4   The area around Loch Druidibeg on South Uist is a National Nature Reserve with many different habitats including freshwater, brackish lagoon, dune, machair, peatland and scrub woodland. The loch itself has many islands, one of which is home to a resident colony of herons. The greylag geese which breed around the Loch contribute to the resident population that remain in the Uists all year. Birds of prey hunting in the reserve include golden eagle, hen harriers, kestrel, peregrine and merlin.

5   Kisimul Castle is a sight to behold, situated in the bay of Castlebay Village on Barra. The stronghold of the MacNeils of Barra, this is the only surviving medieval castle in the Hebrides. Day tickets to visit the castle can be obtained at the local Tourist Information Centre.

ACTIVITIES

6   There are five golf courses in the Hebrides: Barra, Uist, Benbecula, Harris and Lewis. The 9-hole course at Scarista on Harris, in particular, is legendary for its stunning setting and challenging situation. The small greens, massive sand dunes and ever-present Atlantic winds combine for an enjoyable round!

7   The surf around the Hebrides is so good it has put the area on the map for international lovers of the sport. With over 70 beaches, it really is a surfer's paradise. The Isle of Lewis receives swells from almost every direction and is classed as having the most consistent surf in Europe. But with beaches on every coast you are sure to be guaranteed surf no matter what direction the swell is coming from.

8   With some of the most beautiful coastline in Britain, the Hebrides is the perfect wilderness to explore by kayak. See otters, dolphins and puffins as you glide through the crystal clear waters around the islands. The coastline is a labyrinth of complex bays, inlets, dramatic cliffs, secret coves, sandy beaches and offshore islands.... a sea paddler's paradise.

9   The Outer Hebrides is a game angler's dream location. Whether you are a solitary angler, form part of a larger group or are simply looking for a tranquil family vacation, the Outer Hebrides has it all - namely, some of the best summer salmon and trout fishing in Europe.

DON'T MISS

1   **Skara Brae**, 19 miles from Kirkwall, is an unrivalled example of life in Stone Age Orkney. Without doubt the best preserved village in western Europe, the houses contain stone beds, dressers, hearths and drains, giving a fantastic insight into how life was 5,000 years ago. Together with several other historical sites, it is part of a designated World Heritage Site.

2   Discovered in 1958, the **Tomb of the Eagles** is a 5,000 year old tomb containing ceremonial tools, beds, talons and other bones of the white-tailed eagle, pottery and working tools.

3   In the heart of Orkney's main town, Kirkwall, lies **St Magnus Cathedral**. It was built in 1137 by Earl Rognvald, in memory of his cousin Magnus who was earlier murdered by another cousin, Haakon, co-ruler at that time. Today the beautiful sandstone building continues to be a place of worship for the local people.

4   **The Pier Arts Centre** was reopened in 2007 and houses a remarkable collection of 20th century British art. The Collection charts the development of modern art in Britain and includes key work by Barbara Hepworth, Ben Nicholson and Naum Gabo amongst others.

5   Orkney is blessed with an abundance of birds and marine wildlife. Late spring sees the arrival of thousands of breeding seabirds including everybody's favourite the colourful, clown-like puffin. Grey seals breed in huge numbers around the coast in late autumn, while whales, dolphins and porpoise are a regular sight off-shore throughout the summer. **Wildlife** is everywhere, and with a diverse range of professional guiding services there is something to suit everyone.

HISTORY AND HERITAGE

6   The **Ring of Brodgar** and the **Standing Stones of Stenness** are also included within the World Heritage Site. Undeniably mystical, these spiritual places reward visitors with a real sense of ancient times.

7   **Maeshowe** is a central feature of the Neolithic Orkney World Heritage Site. A chambered cairn, it is considered to be one of the finest architectural achievements of its time, around 5,000 years ago. Timed ticketing is in operation, ensuring lots of room and allowing the informative guides to point out all the interesting aspects of the site.

8   The **Broch of Gurness** at Aikerness is a well-organised Iron Age village, giving fascinating insight into community life 2,000 years ago.

9   Travel across the first of the Churchill Barriers to see an artistic phenomenon at the **Italian Chapel**. Built by Italian POWs in WWII, using only the most modest of materials, the intricate interior is all the more impressive.

DON'T MISS

1   Shetland's **local produce** has a reputation for being fresh, natural and good quality. From succulent Shetland smoked salmon to delicious hill lamb, Shetland's food suppliers are at your service.

2   Take a late evening trip to see the **storm petrels**, abundant visitors during the summer. Very small and generally black with a white rump, they can be seen fluttering low over the water pausing momentarily to dip and feed from the surface. They are said to have taken their name from *St Peter* as they appear to be able to walk on water.

3   Shetland is famous amongst those in the know as the place to enjoy sensational **seabird colonies**. If you want close-up views of tens of thousands of breeding gannets, alongside guillemots, puffins, razorbills, kittiwakes, and fulmars, then head for Sumburgh Head, Noss or Hermaness Nature Reserves. These three large seabird colonies are easily accessible and you may well see the famously rare great skuas, or the equally feisty arctic skua.

4   Shetland offers some of the finest **walking** in Europe. The combination of spectacular coastal scenery, quiet inland lochs, and gentle heathery hills is unsurpassed. The walker has the rare opportunity to discover ancient historical sites, dating back to Neolithic times, and observe a wonderful array of wildlife.

5   Officially described as 'one of the most remarkable archaeological sites ever excavated in the British Isles', **Jarlshof** came to light 100 years ago when storms exposed stonework above the beach at the West Voe of Sumburgh. Take a walk through the millenia at this extraordinarily well preserved site, from a Stone Age hut through an Iron Age broch and wheelhouses to a sizeable Viking village and medieval farmstead.

6   Take a trip to **Foula** – one of Britain's most remote inhabited islands. Gaze at the breathtaking 1,200 ft sheer drop at the back of the Kame, said to be one of the highest sea-cliffs in Britain. The name means 'Bird Island' in Old Norse and Foula is designated as a Special Protection Area for birds, a National Scenic Area and a Site of Special Scientific Interest for its plants, birds and geology. This island leaves a lasting impression on everyone who visits.

ATTRACTIONS

7   The broch, or fortified Iron Age tower, on the little island of Mousa is the only one in the world to have survived almost complete for more than 2,000 years. Built as a refuge against raiding local tribes, **Mousa Broch** is one of the wonders of European archaeology - and also ornithology. Tiny storm petrels nest in its stone, visiting the broch only after dark - a night excursion to hear their eerie calls is an experience not to be missed.

8   One of the best places to enjoy the cliff scenery by road is **Eshaness** lighthouse, perched above a precipice of volcanic lava. A short walk away is an impressive collapsed cave, Da Hols o' Scraada (the Devil's Caves). Nearby is Da Grind o' da Navir (Gate of the Borer), a huge gateway in the cliffs where the sea has ripped out a chunk of rock and hurled it inland, and the Loch of Houlland, where the ruin of one of the parish's many brochs provides an excellent example of Iron Age architecture.

9   At **Old Scatness Broch**, next to Sumburgh Airport, a recent archaeological dig revealed one of Britain's most exciting Iron Age villages, with many buildings standing at or near roof height and some still even 'decorated' with yellow clay! Buried for nearly 2,000 years, the site is rich in artefacts and remarkably well preserved.

10 **St Ninian's Isle** became famous in 1958, when a schoolboy helping at an archaeological dig on the island discovered a hoard of silver bowls and ornaments believed to date from around 800AD. Now inhabited only by sheep St Ninian's Isle is a beautiful spot for swimming, picnics and walking. Visit the lovely beach and discover the ruins of the old Celtic chapel.

MAP

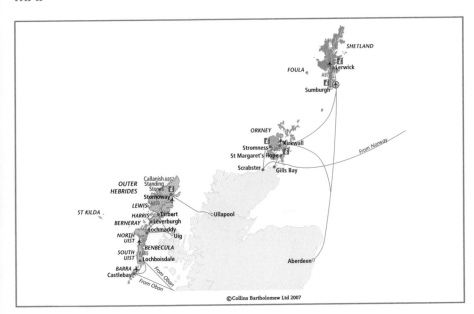

©Collins Bartholomew Ltd 2007

TOURIST INFORMATION CENTRES

Orkney	
Kirkwall	6 Broad Street, Kirkwall KW15 1DH
Stromness	Ferry Terminal Building, Pier Head, Stromness, Orkney KW16 3AA
Shetland	
Lerwick	Market Cross, Lerwick, Shetland ZE1 0LU
Sumburgh Airport	Wilshess Terminal, Sumburgh Airport, Shetland ZE3 9JP
Outer Hebrides	
Stornoway	26 Cromwell Street, Stornoway, Isle of Lewis HS1 2DD

Make the most of your stay in Scotland and make your first stop the Tourist Information Centre wherever you go.

Knowledgeable and friendly staff can help you with information and advice; they can answer your questions, book accommodation and you can even pick up some souvenirs to take home for friends and family.

For information and ideas about exploring Scotland in advance of your trip, call our booking and information service or go to **www.visitscotland.com**

Call **0845 22 55 121**

or if calling from outside the UK call **+44 (0) 1506 832 121**

From Ireland call **1800 932 510**

A £4 booking fee applies to telephone bookings of accommodation.

64581

Laxdale, Isle of Lewis, Western Isles   Map Ref: 3D4

Laxdale Holiday Park

6 Laxdale Lane, Laxdale, Isle of Lewis, HS2 0DR
Tel:01851 706966/703234
Email:info@laxdaleholidaypark.com
Web:www.laxdaleholidaypark.com

2 acres, mixed, Jan-Dec, Extra charge for electricty, showers, awnings.

Park accommodation: **43**

13 tourers £9.00-11.00, 13 motors £9.00-11.00, 30 tents £7.50-10.00, Total Touring Pitches 43.

4 Holiday Caravans to let, sleeps 4-6, total sleeping capacity 24, £170.00-250.00 per week.

From Stornoway take A857 for 1ml. Park is 2nd left after hospital. Signposted.

Callanish Standing Stones, Isle of Lewis

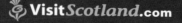

Abington

Mount View Caravan Park
Station Road
Abington
South Lanarkshire
ML12 6RW
Tel: 01864 502808
★★★★ Holiday Park

by Acharacle

Resipole Farm Caravan Park
Loch Sunart
by Acharacle
Argyll
PH36 4HX
Tel: 01967 431235
★★★★ Holiday Park

Annan

Queensberry Bay Caravan Park
Powfoot
Annan
Dumfriesshire
DG12 5PU
Tel: 01461 700205
★★★★ Holiday Park

Appin

Appin Holiday Homes
Appin
Argyll
PA38 4BQ
Tel: 01631 730287
★★★★ Holiday Park

Ayr

Craig Tara
Dunure Road
Ayr
Ayrshire
KA7 4LB
Tel: 01292 265141
★★★★ Holiday Park

by Ayr

Croft Head Caravan Park
by Ayr
KA6 6EN
Tel: 01292 263516
★★★★ Holiday Park

Sundrum Castle Holiday Park
Coylton
by Ayr
Ayrshire
KA6 6HX
Tel: 01292 570057(Tourers)
Tel: 0191 2759098 (Statics)
★★★★ Holiday Park

Blair Atholl

Blair Castle Caravan Park
Blair Atholl
Perthshire
PH18 5SR
Tel: 01796 481263
★★★★★ Holiday Park

Blairgowrie

Blairgowrie Holiday Park
Rattray
Blairgowrie
Perthshire
PH10 7AL
Tel: 01250 876666
★★★★★ Holiday Park

Five Roads Caravan Park
by Alyth
Blairgowrie
Perthshire
PH11 8NB
Tel: 01828 632255
★★★★ Holiday Park

by Blairgowrie

Corriefodly Holiday Park
Bridge of Cally
by Blairgowrie
Perthshire
PH10 7JG
Tel: 01250 886236
★★★★★ Holiday Park

Boat of Garten

Boat of Garten Holiday Park
Desmar Road
Boat of Garten
PH24 3BN
Tel: 01479 831652
★★★★ Holiday Park

Cairnryan

Cairnryan Caravan Park
Cairnryan
Wigtownshire
DG9 8QX
Tel: 01581 200231
★★★★ Holiday Park

Coldingham

Scoutscroft Holiday Centre
St Abbs Road
Coldingham
Berwickshire
TD14 5NB
Tel: 01890 771338 and
Tel: 01890 771534
★★★★★ Holiday Park

Crail

Sauchope Links Caravan Park
Crail
Fife
KY10 3XJ
Tel: 01333 870446
★★★★★ Holiday Park

Crianlarich

Glendochart Caravan Park
Luib
Crianlarich
Perthshire
FK20 8QT
Tel: 01567 820637
★★★★ Holiday Park

Crieff

Braidhaugh Park
South Bridgend
Crieff
Perthshire
PH7 4HP
Tel: 01764 652951
★★★★ Holiday Park

Crocketford

Park of Brandedleys
Crocketford
Dumfriesshire
DG2 8RG
Tel: 01387 266700
★★★★ Holiday Park

Dalbeattie

Glenearly Caravan Park
Park Farm
Dalbeattie
Kirkcudbrightshire
DG5 4NE
Tel: 01556 611393
★★★★ Holiday Park

Dornoch

**Dornoch Caravan &
Camping Park**
The Links
Dornoch
Sutherland
IV25 3LX
Tel: 01862 810423
★★★★ Holiday Park

by Dalbeattie

Sandyhills Bay Leisure Park
Sandyhills
by Dalbeattie
Kirkcudbrightshire
DG5 4NY
Tel: 01387 780257
★★★★ Holiday Park

Dornoch

**Grannies Heilan Hame
Holiday Park**
Embo
Dornoch
Sutherland
IV25 3QD
Tel: 01862 810383
★★★★ Holiday Park

Dornoch

Pitgrudy Caravan Park
Poles Road
Dornoch
Sutherland
IV25 3HY
Tel: 01862 821253/810001
★★★★ Holiday Park

Dunbar

Belhaven Bay Caravan Park
Belhaven Bay
Dunbar
East Lothian
EH42 1TU
Tel: 01368 865956
★★★★ Holiday Park

**Thurston Manor
Holiday Home Park**
Innerwick
Dunbar
East Lothian
EH42 1SA
Tel: 01368 840643
★★★★★ Holiday Park

Dunkeld

Erigmore House Holiday Park
Birnam
Dunkeld
Perthshire
PH8 0BJ
Tel: 01350 727236
★★★★ Holiday Park

Dunoon

Hunters Quay Holiday Village
Hunters Quay
Dunoon
Argyll
PA23 8HP
Tel: 01369 707772
★★★★★ Holiday Park

Edinburgh

Mortonhall Caravan Park
38 Mortonhall Gate, Frogston
Road East
Edinburgh
EH16 6TJ
Tel: 0131 664 1533
★★★★ Holiday Park

Evanton

Black Rock Caravan Park
Balconie Street
Evanton
Ross-shire
IV16 9UN
Tel: 01349 830917
★★★★★ Holiday Park

Eyemouth

Eyemouth Holiday Park
Fort Road
Eyemouth
Berwickshire
TD14 5BE
Tel: 01890 751050
★★★★ Holiday Park

Fintry

Balgair Castle Caravan Park
Overglinns
Fintry
Stirlingshire
G63 0LP
Tel: 01360 860283
★★★★ Holiday Park

Gairloch

Sands Holiday Centre
Gairloch
Ross-shire
IV21 2DL
Tel: 01445 712152
★★★★ Holiday Park

Gartmore

Trossachs Holiday Park
Gartmore
Stirling
FK8 3SA
Tel: 01877 382614
★★★★★ Holiday Park

Gatehouse of Fleet

Auchenlarie Holiday Park
Gatehouse of Fleet
Castle Douglas
DG7 2EX
Tel: 01557 840251
★★★★ Holiday Park

Girvan

Bennane Shore Holiday Park
Lendalfoot
Girvan
Ayrshire
KA26 0JG
Tel: 01465 891233
★★★★★ Holiday Park

Glencoe

Invercoe
Caravan & Camping Park
Invercoe
Glencoe
Argyll
PH49 4HP
Tel: 01855 811210
★★★★★ Holiday Park

Glendaruel

Glendaruel Caravan Park
Glendaruel
Argyll
PA22 3AB
Tel: 01369 820267
★★★★★ Holiday Park

Glenluce

Glenluce
Caravan & Camping Park
Glenluce
Wigtownshire
DG8 0QR
Tel: 01581 300412
★★★★ Holiday Park

Whitecairn Farm Caravan Park
Whitecairn
Glenluce
Wigtownshire
DG8 0NZ
Tel: 01581 300267
★★★★ Holiday Park

by Helensburgh

Rosneath Castle
Caravan Park Ltd
Rosneath
by Helensburgh
Argyll & Bute
G84 0QS
Tel: 01436 831208/831391
★★★★★ Holiday Park

Huntly

Huntly Castle Caravan Park
The Meadows
Huntly
Aberdeenshire
AB54 4UJ
Tel: 01466 794999
★★★★★ Holiday Park

Inveraray

Argyll Caravan Park
Inveraray
Argyll
PA32 8XT
Tel: 01499 302285
★★★★★ Holiday Park

Jedburgh

Jedwater Caravan Park
Jedburgh
Roxburghshire
TD8 6PJ
Tel: 01835 869595
★★★★ Holiday Park

by Kennoway

Letham Feus Caravan Park
Cupar Road
by Kennoway
Fife
KY8 4HR
Tel: 01333 351900
★★★★ Holiday Park

Kintyre

Carradale Bay Caravan Park
Carradale
Kintyre
Argyll
PA28 6QG
Tel: 01583 431665
★★★★ Holiday Park

Kippford

Kippford Holiday Park
Kippford
Kirkcudbrightshire
DG5 4LF
Tel: 01556 620636
★★★★★ Holiday Park

Kirkcudbright

Brighouse Bay Holiday Park
Borgue Road
Kirkcudbright
Kirkcudbrightshire
DG6 4TS
Tel: 01557 870267
★★★★★ Holiday Park

Seaward Caravan Park
Dhoon Bay
Kirkcudbright
Kirkcudbrighshire
DG6 4TJ
Tel: 01557 331079
★★★★ Holiday Park

Loch Lomond

Lomond Woods Holiday Park
Balloch
Loch Lomond
Dunbartonshire
G83 8QP
Tel: 01389 755000
★★★★★ Holiday Park

Lochgoilhead

Drimsynie & Kingfisher Holiday Village
Drimsynie Estate
Lochgoilhead
Argyll
PA24 8AD
Tel: 01301 703312
★★★★ Holiday Park

Longniddry

Seton Sands Holiday Village
Links Road, Longniddry
Longniddry
East Lothian
EH32 0QF
Tel: 01875 813333
★★★★ Holiday Park

Lossiemouth

Silver Sands Leisure Park
Covesea, West Beach
Lossiemouth
Morayshire
IV31 6SP
Tel: 01343 813262
★★★★ Holiday Park

by Luss

Inverbeg Holiday Park
Inverbeg
by Luss
Dunbartonshire
G83 8PD
Tel: 01436 860267
★★★★ Holiday Park

Macduff

Myrus Holiday Park
Myrus Crossroads
Macduff
by Banff
AB45 3QP
★★★★★ Holiday Park

Maryculter

Lower Deeside Holiday Park
South Deeside Road
Maryculter
Aberdeenshire
AB12 5FX
Tel: 01224 733860
★★★★ Holiday Park

Monifieth

Riverview Caravan Park
Marine Drive
Monifieth, by Dundee
Angus
DD5 4NN
Tel: 01382 817979
★★★★★ Holiday Park

Nairn

Nairn Lochloy Holiday Park
East Beach
Nairn
Nairnshire
IV12 4PH
Tel: 01667 453764
★★★★ Holiday Park

Newton Stewart

Luce Bay Holiday Park & Lodges
Auchenmalg
Newton Stewart
Wigtownshire
DG8 0JT
Tel: 01581 500227
★★★★ Holiday Park

Three Lochs Holiday Park
Balminnoch
Newton Stewart
Wigtownshire
DG8 0EP
Tel: 01671 830304
★★★★ Holiday Park

nr Newton Stewart

Creetown Caravan Park
Silver Street, Creetown
nr Newton Stewart
Wigtownshire
DG8 7HU
Tel: 01671 820377
★★★★ Holiday Park

North Berwick

Tantallon Caravan Park
Dunbar Road
North Berwick
East Lothian
EH39 5NJ
Tel: 01620 893348
★★★★ Holiday Park

by Oban

Tralee Bay
Purple Thistle Holidays
Benderloch
by Oban
Argyll
PA37 1QR
Tel: 01631 720255
★★★★★ Holiday Park

Pitlochry

Milton of Fonab Caravan Park
Bridge Road
Pitlochry
Perthshire
PH16 5NA
Tel: 01796 472882
★★★★ Holiday Park

The River Tilt Park
Bridge of Tilt, Blair Atholl
Pitlochry
Perthshire
PH18 5TE
Tel: 01796 481467
★★★★★ Holiday Park

nr Pitlochry

Tummel Valley Holiday Park
nr Pitlochry
Perthshire
PH16 5SA
Tel: 01882 634221
★★★★ Holiday Park

by Portsoy

Sandend Caravan Park
Sandend
by Portsoy
Banffshire
AB4 2UA
Tel: 01261 842660
★★★★ Holiday Park

Southerness

Southerness Holiday Village
Southerness
Dumfriesshire
DG2 8AZ
Tel: 01387 880256
★★★★ Holiday Park

St Andrews

Clayton Caravan Park
St Andrews
Fife
KY16 9YB
Tel: 01334 870242
★★★★ Holiday Park

Stornoway

Laxdale Holiday Park
6 Laxdale Lane, Laxdale
Stornoway
Lewis, Western Isles
HS2 0DR
Tel: 01851 706966/703234
★★★★ Touring Park

Stranraer

Drumlochart Caravan Park
Lochnaw, Leswalt
Stranraer
Wigtownshire
DG9 0RN
Tel: 01776 870232
★★★★★ Holiday Park

Sands of Luce Holiday Park
Sandhead
Stranraer
Wigtownshire
DG9 9JN
Tel: 01776 830456
★★★★ Holiday Park

Tarbet

Loch Lomond Holiday Park
Inveruglas
Tarbet
Argyll & Bute
G83 7DW
Tel: 01301 704224
★★★★★ Holiday Park

Wemyss Bay

Wemyss Bay Holiday Park
Wemyss Bay
Renfrewshire
PA18 6BA
Tel: 01475 520812
★★★★ Holiday Park

Aberdeen

Aberdeen Youth Hostel
8 Queens Road
Aberdeen
AB10 4ZT
Tel: 01224 646988
★★★★ Hostel

Aberfeldy

The Bunkhouse
Glassie Farm
Aberfeldy
Perthshire
PH15 2JN
Tel: 01887 820265
★★★★ Hostel

by Aberfoyle

Inversnaid Bunkhouse
Inversnaid
by Aberfoyle
Stirlingshire
FK8 3TU
Tel: 01301 702970
Bunkhouse

Alexandria

Loch Lomond Youth Hostel
Arden
Alexandria
Dunbartonshire
G83 8RB
Tel: 01389 850226
★★★ Hostel

Isle of Arran, Lochranza

Lochranza Youth Hostel
Lochranza
KA27 8HL
Tel: 01770 830631
★★★ Hostel

Isle of Arran, Kilmory

Kilmory Lodge Bunkhouse
Isle of Arran
Kilmory
KA27 8PQ
Tel: 01770 870345
★★★ Group Accommodation

Aviemore

Aviemore Bunkhouse
Dalfaber Road
Aviemore
Inverness-shire
PH22 1PU
Tel: 01479 811181
★★★★ Hostel

Aviemore Youth Hostel
25 Grampian Road
Aviemore
Inverness-shire
PH22 1PR
Tel: 0871 330 8504
★★★★ Hostel

Alltnacriche
Lynwilg
Aviemore
PH22 1PZ
Tel: 01479 810237
★★★ Group Accommodation

Cairngorm Lodge (Loch Morlich)
Aviemore
PH22 1QY
Tel: 0871 330 8538
★★★★ Hostel

Ballachulish

Glencoe Independent Hostel
Glencoe
Ballachulish
Argyll
PH49 4HX
Tel: 01855 811906
Bunkhouse

Glencoe Youth Hostel
Glencoe
Ballachulish
Argyll
PA39 4HX
Tel: 01855 811219
★★★ Hostel

Banavie

Chase the Wild Goose Hostel
Lochiel Cresent
Banavie
Fort William
PH33 7LY
Tel: 01397 772531
★★★★ Hostel

Isle of Barra, Castlebay

Dunard Hostel
Isle of Barra
Castlebay
HS9 5XA
Tel: 01871 810443
★★★★ Hostel

by Blairgowrie

Gulabin Lodge
Spittal of Glenshee
by Blairgowrie
Perthshire
PH10 7QE
Tel: 01250 885255
★★ Activity Accommodation

Boat of Garten

Fraoch Lodge
Deshar Road
Boat of Garten
PH24 3BN
Tel: 01479 831331
★★★★ Hostel

Braemar

Braemar Lodge Bunkhouse
Glenshee Road
Braemar
AB35 5YQ
Tel: 013397 41627
★★★★ Hostel

Braemar Youth Hostel
Corrie Feragie, 21 Glenshee Road
Braemar
AB35 2QL
Tel: 01339 741659
★★★ Hostel

Rucksacks
15 Mar Road
Braemar
AB35 5YL
Tel: 01339 74157
Bunkhouse

by Braemar

Inverey Youth Hostel
Aberdeenshire
by Braemar
AB35 5YB
Tel: 01339 741017
★ Hostel

Bridge of Orchy

The West Highland Way Sleeper
Bridge of Orchy Railway Station
Bridge of Orchy
Argyll
PA36 4AD
Tel: 01838 400548
★★★ Hostel

Callander

Trossachs Backpackers
Invertrossachs Road
Callander
FK17 8HW
Tel: 01877 331200
★★★★ Hostel

nr Callander

Sir Andrew Murray House
Strathayre
nr Callandar
Stirlingshire
FK18 8NQ
Tel: 01324 562452
★★★ Group Accommodation

Cannich, Beauly

Glen Affric Youth Hostel
Allt Beithe, Glen Affric
Cannich
Inverness-shire
IV4 7NO
Tel:
★ Hostel

Caputh, Perth

Wester Caputh Lodge
Manse Road
Caputh
Perthshire
PH1 4JH
Tel: 01738 710449
★★★★ Hostel

Carbost

But n Ben
7 Portnalong
Carbost
Isle of Skye
IV42 8SL
Tel: 01478 640254
★★★★ Hostel

Croft Bunkhouse
7 Portnalong
Carbost
Isle of Skye
IV42 8SL
Tel: 01478 640254
★★★ Hostel

Glenbrittle Youth Hostel
Glenbrittle
Carbost
Isle of Skye
IV47 8TA
Tel: 01478 640278
★★★ Hostel

The Waterfront Bunkhouse
The Old Inn
Carbost
Isle of Skye
IV47 8SR
Tel: 01478 640205
★★★ Hostel

Carrbridge

Slochd Mhor Lodge
Slochd
Carrbridge
Inverness-shire
PH23 3AY
Tel: 01479 841666
★★★★ Hostel

Carrbridge Bunkhouse Hostel
Dalrachney House
Carrbridge
PH23 3AX
Tel: 01479 841250
★★★ Hostel

Castle Douglas

Galloway Sailing Centre
Loch Ken
Castle Douglas
DG7 3WQ
Tel: 01644 720626
★★★ Activity Accommodation

by Castle Douglas

Kendoon Youth Hostel
Dalry
by Castle Douglas
DG7 3UD
Tel: 01644 460680
★ Hostel

Coldingham

Coldingham Youth Hostel
Coldingham Sands
Coldingham
Berwickshire
TD14 5PA
Tel: 0870 004 1111/
0870 155 3255
★★★ Hostel

Isle of Colonsay

Colonsay Keepers Backpackers Lodge
Argyll
PA61 7YU
Tel: 01951 200312
★★ Hostel

Crianlarich

Crianlarich Youth Hostel
Station Road
Crianlarich
FK20 8QN
Tel: 0871 330 8513
★★★ Hostel

by Crieff

Comrie Croft Hostel
Braincroft, Comrie Road
by Crieff
PH7 4JZ
Tel: 01764 670140
★★★★ Hostel

Culrain

Carbisdale Castle Youth Hostel
Culrain
Sutherland
IV24 3DP
Tel: 01549 921232
★★★★ Hostel

Dollar

Glendevon Youth Hostel
Glendevon Village
Dollar
Clackmannanshire
FK14 7JY
Tel: 01259 740121
★★ Hostel

Drumnadrochit

Loch Ness Backpackers Lodge
East Lewiston
Drumnadrochit
IV3 6UJ
Tel: 01456 450807
★★★ Hostel

by Drymen

Rowardennan Youth Hostel
Rowardennan
by Drymen
G63 0AR
0871 330 8548
★★★★ Hostel

Dumfries

Marthrown of Mabie
Mabie Forest
Dumfries
DG2 8HB
Tel: 01387 247900
★★★ Hostel

Dundonnell

Sail Mhor Croft Hostel
Camusnagaul
Dundonnell
IV23 2QT
Tel: 01854 633224
★★★ Hostel

Badrallach Bothy
Ross-shire
Dundonnell
IV23 2QP
Tel: 01854 633281
Bothy

by Dunoon

Bernice Farmhouse & Cottage
Bernice
by Dunoon
Argyll
PA23 8QX
Tel: 01369 706337
★★ up to ★★★★
Group Accommodation

Durness

Lazy Crofter
Durine
Durness
Sutherland
IV27 4PN
Tel: 01971 511202
★★★ Hostel

Edinburgh

Argyle Backpackers Hotel
14 Argyle Place
Edinburgh
EH9 1JL
Tel: 0131 667 9991
★★ Backpackers

Belford Hostel
6-8 Douglas Gardens
Edinburgh
EH4 3DA
Tel: 0131 225 6209
★★★ Hostel

Brodies 1
12 High Street Royal Mile
Edinburgh
EH1 1TB
Tel: 0131 556 6770
★★ Hostel

Brodies 2
93 High Street, The Royal Mile
Edinburgh
Lothian
EH1 1SG
Tel: 0131 5562223
★★★ Hostel

Edinburgh continued

Budget Backpackers
15 Cowgatehead
Edinburgh
EH1 1JY
Tel: 0131 226 6351
★★★ Hostel

Budget Backpackers
37-39 Cowgate
Edinburgh
EH1 1JR
Tel: 0131 226 6351
★★★★ Backpackers

Castle Rock Hostel
15 Johnston Terrace
Edinburgh
EH1 2PW
Tel: 0131 225 9666
★★ Backpackers

Cowgate Hostel
94 - 116 Cowgate
Edinburgh
EH1 1JN
Tel: 0131 226 2153
★★ Backpackers

Edinburgh Backpackers
65 Cockburn Street
Edinburgh
EH1 1BU
Tel: 0131 220 1717
★★★ Hostel

Edinburgh Central Youth Hostel
9 Haddington Place
Edinburgh
Midlothian
EH7 4AL
Tel: 0131 524
★★★★★ Hostel

Euro Hostels Limited
Darroch Court
Edinburgh
EH8 9TS
Tel: 08454 900461
★★★ Hostel

**THE GLOBETROTTER INN
EDINBURGH Limited**
Cramond Foreshore
Marine Drive
Edinburgh
Lothian
EH4 5EP
Tel: 0131 3361030
★★★★ Hostel

High Street Hostel
8 Blackfriars Street
Edinburgh
EH1 1NE
Tel: 0131 557 3984
★★ Backpackers

Royal Mile Backpackers
105 High Street
Edinburgh
EH1 1SG
Tel: 0131 557 6120
★★ Backpackers

St Christophers Inn
9-13 Market Street
Edinburgh
EH1 1DE
Tel: 0131 226 1446
★★★ Backpackers

Smart City Hostel
50 Blackfriars Street
Edinburgh
EH1 1NE
★★★★★ Hostel

Westend Hostel
3 Clifton Terrace
Edinburgh
Lothian
EH12 5DR
Tel: 0131 313 1031
★★★ Hostel

Isle of Eigg

Glebe Barn
Isle of Eigg
PH42 4RL
Tel: 01687 482417
★★★★ Hostel

Fearnan

Culdees Bunkhouse
Boreland Farm
Fearnan
Perthshire
PH15 2PG
Tel: 01887 830519
★★★ Hostel

Fort Augustus

Morags Lodge
Bunnoich Brae
Fort Augustus
PH32 4DG
Tel: 01320 366289
★★★★ Hostel

Fort William

Achintee Farm Hostel
Fort William
PH33 6TE
Tel: 01397 702240
★★ Hostel

Bank Street Lodge
Bank Street
Fort William
Inverness-shire
PH33 6AY
Tel: 01397 700070
★★★ Hostel

Ben Nevis Inn
Achintee
Fort William
PH33 6TE
Tel: 01397 701227
Bunkhouse

Calluna
Heathercroft
Fort William
PH33 6RE
Tel: 01397 700451
Bunkhouse

Farr Cottage Lodge
Corpach
Fort William
PH33 7LR
Tel: 01397 772315
★★★ Hostel

Fort William Backpackers
Alma Road
Fort William
PH33 6HB
Tel: 01397 700711
★★ Backpackers

Glen Nevis Youth Hostel
Glen Nevis
Fort William
Inverness-shire
PH33 6ST
Tel: 01397 702336
★★★ Hostel

Inchree Lodge
Onich
Fort William
Inverness-shire
PH33 6SE
Tel: 01855 821287
★★★★ Hostel

**The Smiddy Bunkhouse and
Blacksmiths Backpackers Lodge**
Station Road, Corpach
Fort William
Inverness-shire
PH33 7JH
Tel: 01397 772467
★★★ Hostel

by Fort William

Loch Ossian Youth Hostel
Corrour
by Fort William
Inverness-shire
PH30 4AA
Tel: 01397 732207
★★★ Hostel

Gairloch

Carn Dearg Youth Hostel
Carn Dearg
Gairloch
Ross-shire
IV21 2DJ
Tel: 01445 712219
★★★ Hostel

Rua Reidh Lighthouse
Melvaig
Gairloch
Ross-shire
IV21 2EA
Tel: 01445 771263
★★★★ Hostel

Glasgow

Bunkum Backpackers
26 Hillhead Street
Glasgow
G12 8PY
Tel: 0141 581 4481
★★ Hostel

Cairncross House
20 Kelvinhaugh Place
Glasgow
G3 8NH
Tel: 0141 330 5385
★★★ Hostel

Euro Hostels
318 Clyde Street
Glasgow
G1 4NR
Tel: 0141 222 2828
★★★ Hostel

HOSTEL ACCOMMODATION

Glasgow continued

Glades
142 Albert Road, Crosshill
Glasgow
G42 8UF
Tel: 0141 639 2601
★★★★ **Hostel**

Glasgow Youth Hostel
7/8 Park Terrace
Glasgow
G3 6BY
Tel: 0141 332 3004
★★★★ **Hostel**

Globetrotter/Rucksacks
56 Berkeley Street
Charing Cross
Glasgow
G3 7DX
Tel: 0141 221 7880/
0141 204 5470
★★ **Backpackers**

Margaret Macdonald House
89 Buccleuch Street
Glasgow
G3 6QT
Tel: 0141 331 1261
★★ **Hostel**

Murano Street Student Village
13 Caithness Street
Glasgow
G20 7SB
★★★ **Hostel**

Rucksacks
60 Berkeley Street
Glasgow
G3 7DS
Tel: 0141 2045470
★★ **Backpackers**

Glen Clova, By Kirriemuir

The Steading Bunkhouse
Glen Clova Hotel
Glen Clova
Angus
DD8 4QS
Tel: 01575 550 350
★★★ **Hostel**

Glen Urquhart

The Glen Urquhart Hostel
Bearnock
Glen Urquhart
Inverness-shire
IV63 6TN
Tel: 01463 230218
★★★★★ **Hostel**

Glenfinnan

Glenfinnan Sleeping Car
Glenfinnan Station
Glenfinnan
PH37 4LT
Tel: 01347 722295
Bunkhouse

Glenlyon

Ben Lawers Bunkhouse
Milton Eonan, Bridge of Balgie
Glenlyon
Perthshire
PH15 2PT
Tel: 01881 866318
★★★★ **Hostel**

Glenmoriston

Loch Ness Youth Hostel
Glenmoriston
IV63 7XD
Tel: 01320 351274
★★ **Hostel**

Grantown-on-Spey

Ardenbeg Outdoor Centre
Grant Road
Grantown-on-Spey
Moray
PH26 3LD
Tel: 01479 872824
★★★ **Hostel**

Helmsdale

Helmsdale Hostel
Stafford Street
Helmsdale
KW8 6JR
Tel: 01431 821636
★★★★ **Hostel**

Inveraray

Inveraray Youth Hostel
Dalmally Road
Inveraray
PA32 8XD
Tel: 01499 302454
★★★ **Hostel**

Invergarry

Invergarry Lodge
Mandally Road
Invergarry
PH35 4HP
Tel: 01809 501412
★★★★ **Hostel**

Inverness

Bazpackers Hostel
4 Culduthel Road
Inverness
IV2 4AB
Tel: 01463 717663
★★★ **Backpackers**

Eastgate Backpackers Hostel
38 Eastgate
Inverness
IV2 3NA
Tel: 01463 718756
★★★ **Hostel**

Inverness Millburn Youth Hostel
Victoria Drive
Inverness
IV2 3QB
Tel: 0871 330 8529
★★★★ **Hostel**

Inverness Student Hotel
8 Culduthel Road
Inverness
IV2 4AB
Tel: 01463 236556
★★ **Backpackers**

Inverness Tourist Hostel
24 Rose Street
Inverness
IV1 1NQ
Tel: 01463 241962
★★ **Hostel**

Isle of Iona

Iona Hostel
Lagandorain
Isle of Iona
Argyll
PA76 6SW
Tel: 01681 700781
★★★★ **Hostel**

Isle of Islay

Port Charlotte Youth Hostel
Port Charlotte
Isle of Islay
PA48 7TX
Tel: 01496 850385
★★★ **Hostel**

Kelso

Kirk Yetholm Youth Hostel
Kirk Yetholm
Kelso
Roxburghshire
TD5 8PG
Tel: 0870 004 1132/
0870 155 3255
★★ **Hostel**

Killin

Braveheart Backpackers
Lochay Lodge, Killin Hotel
Killin
FK21 8TP
Tel: 01567 829084
Bunkhouse

Killin Youth Hostel
Killin
Perthshire
FK21 8TN
Tel: 0870 0041131
★★★ **Hostel**

Kincraig

Glen Feshie Hostel
Glen Feshie
Kincraig
PH21 1NH
Tel: 01540 651323
Bunkhouse

Kingussie

Happy Days
65 High Street
Kingussie
PH21 1HX
Tel: 01540 661175
★★★★ **Hostel**

Lairds Bothy
68/70 High Street
Kingussie
PH21 1HZ
Tel: 01540 661334
★★★ **Hostel**

nr Kingussie

Lagganlia Outdoor Centre
Kincraig
nr Kingussie
Inverness-shire
PH21 1NG
Tel: 01540 651265
★★ up to ★★★★
Activity Accommodation

Kinlochard

Ledard Farm Bothies
Ledard Farm
Kinlochard
FK8 3TL
Tel: 01877 387219
Bunkhouse

Kinlochewe

Kinlochewe Bunkhouse
Ross-shire
Kinlochewe
IV22 2PA
Tel: 01445 760253
Bunkhouse

Blackwater Hostel
Lab Road
Kinlochewe
PH50 4SG
Tel: 01855 831253
★★★★ **Hostel**
&

Kirriemuir

Glen Prosen Hostel
Glenprosen
Kirriemuir
Angus
DD8 4SA
Tel: 01575 450456
★★★★ **Hostel**

Kyle

Ratagan Youth Hostel
Glenshiel
Kyle
Ross-shire
IV40 8HP
Tel: 0870 0041147
★★★★ **Hostel**

Laggan Bridge

Pottery Bunkhouse
Laggan Bridge
PH20 1BT
Tel: 01528 544231
★★★★ **Hostel**

Lairg

Achmelvich Youth Hostel
Recharn
Lairg
Sutherland
IV27 4JB
Tel: 01571 844480
★ **Hostel**

Durness Youth Hostel
Smoo
Lairg
Sutherland
IV27 4QA
Tel: 01847 891113
Bunkhouse

Inchnadamph Lodge Hostel
Inchnadamph, Elphin
Lairg
Sutherland
IV27 4HL
Tel: 01571 822218
★★★ **Hostel**

Mallaig

Sheenas Backpackers Lodge
Mallaig
Inverness-shire
PH41 4PU
Tel: 01687 462764
★★★ **Hostel**

Melrose

Melrose Youth Hostel
Priorwood
Melrose
TD6 9EF
Tel: 01896 822521
★★★ **Hostel**

Isle of Mull, Dervaig

Dervaig Bunkrooms
Dervaig Village Hall
Dervaig
Isle of Mull
PA75 6JN
Tel: 01688 400491
Bunkhouse

Isle of Mull, Tobermory

Tobermory Youth Hostel
Main Street
Tobermory
Isle of Mull
PA75 6NU
Tel: 01688 302481
★★★★ **Hostel**

Nethy Bridge

Nethy Station
Station Road
Nethy Bridge
PH25 3DN
Tel: 01479 821370
★★ **Group Accommodation**

Lazy Duck Hostel
Nethy Bridge
PH25 3ED
Tel: 01479 821642
★★★★ **Hostel**

New Lanark, by Lanark

New Lanark Youth Hostel
Wee Row, Rosedale Street
New Lanark
ML11 9DJ
Tel: 01555 666710
★★★ **Hostel**

Newton Stewart

Minnigaff Youth Hostel
Wigtownshire
Newton Stewart
DG8 6PL
Tel: 01671 402211
★★ **Hostel**

Newtonmore

Craigower Lodge
Golf Course Road
Newtonmore
Inverness-shire
PH20 1AT
08450 505052
★★★
Activity Accommodation
&

Newtonmore Hostel
Craigellachie House
Newtonmore
Inverness-shire
PH20 1DA
Tel: 01540 673360
★★★ **Hostel**

Strathspey Mountain Hostel
Main Street
Newtonmore
Inverness-shire
PH20 1DR
Tel: 01540 673694
★★★ **Hostel**
&

Oban

Corran House Hostel
1 Victoria Crescent
Oban
Argyll
PA34 5PN
Tel: 01631 566040
★★★★ **Hostel**

Jeremy Inglis Hostel
21 Airds Crescent
Oban
Argyll
PA34 4BA
Tel: 01631 565065
★ **Hostel**

Oban continued

Oban Backpackers
Breadalbane Street
Oban
Argyll
PA34 5NZ
Tel: 01631 562107
★★ **Backpackers**

Oban Youth Hostel
Esplanade
Oban
PA34 5AF
Tel: 0871 330 8545
★★★★ **Hostel**

Onich

Corran Bunkhouse
Corran
Onich
Fort William
PH33 6SE
Tel: 01855 821000
★★★★ **Hostel**

Inchree Hostel
Onich
Fort William
PH33 6SE
Tel: 01855 821287
★★★ **Group Accommodation**

Orkney, Birsay

Birsay Outdoor Centre
(A966)
Birsay
Orkney
KW17 2LY
Tel: 01856 873535
★★★ **Hostel**

Orkney, Hoy

Hoy Centre
Moaness
Hoy
Orkney
KW15 3NJ
Tel: 01856 873535
★★★★ **Hostel**

Rackwick Outdoor Centre
N/A B9047
Hoy
KW16 3NJ
Tel: 01856 873535
★★★ **Hostel**

Orkney, Kirkwall

Kirkwall Youth Hostel
Old Scapa Road
Kirkwall
Orkney
KW15 1BB
Tel: 0871 330 8533
★★ **Hostel**

Peedie Hostel
Ayre Road
Kirkwall
Orkney
KW15 1QX
Tel: 01556 875477
★★★ **Hostel**

Orkney, Rousay

Rousay Hostel
Trumland Farm
Rousay
Orkney
KW17 2PU
Tel: 01856 821252
★★★ **Hostel**

Orkney, Sanday

Ayres Rock Hostel
Ayre
Sanday
Orkney
KW17 2AY
Tel: 01857 600410
★★★★ **Hostel**

Orkney, Stromness

Brown's Hostel
45/47 Victoria Street
Stromness
KW16 3BS
Tel: 01856 850661
★★★ **Hostel**

Hamnavoe Hostel
10a North End Rd
Stromness
Orkney
KW16 3AG
Tel: 01856 850661
★★★★ **Hostel**

Stromness Hostel
Hellihole Road
Stromness
Orkney
KW16 3DE
Tel: 01856 850870
★★★ **Hostel**

Orkney, Twingness

The Observatory Hostel
Twingness
North Ronaldsay
KW17 2BE
Tel: 01857 633200
★★★★ **Hostel**

Orkney, South Ronaldsay

Wheems Bothy
East Side
South Ronaldsay
Orkney
KW17 2TJ
Tel: 01856 831537
Bunkhouse

Orkney, St Margarets Hope

St Margarets Hope Backpackers
Back Road
St Margarets Hope
Orkney
KW17 2SR
Tel: 01856 831225
★★★ **Backpackers**

Orkney, Westray

Bis Geos Hostel
Westray
Orkney
KW17 2DW
Tel: 01857 677420
★★★★★ **Hostel**

The Barn
Chalmersquoy
Orkney
KW17 2BZ
Tel: 01857 677214
★★★★ **Hostel**

Pitlochry

Pitlochry Backpackers
134 Atholl Road
Pitlochry
Perthshire
PH16 5AB
Tel: 01796 470044
★★★ **Hostel**

Pitlochry Youth Hostel
Braeknowe, Knockard Road
Pitlochry
Perthshire
PH16 5HJ
Tel: 01796 472308
★★★ **Hostel**

Plockton

Plockton Station
Burnside
Plockton
IV52 8TF
Tel: 01599 544235
Bunkhouse

Raasay

Raasay Youth Hostel
Creachan Cottage
Raasay
By Kyle
IV40 8NT
Tel: 01478 660240
★★★ **Hostel**

Rattray, Peterhead

Rattray Head Hostel
Lighthouse Cottages
Rattray
Aberdeenshire
AB42 3HA
Tel: 01346 532236
★★ **Hostel**

Rogart

Sleeperzzz.com
Rogart
IV28 3XA
Tel: 01408 641343
★★★

Roy Bridge

Grey Corrie Lodge
Inverness-shire
Roy Bridge
PH31 4AN
Tel: 01397 712236
Bunkhouse

Selkirk

Broadmeadows Youth Hostel
Old Broadmeadow
Yarrowford
Selkirk
TD7 5LZ
Tel: 0870 004 1107/
0870 155 3255
★★ **Hostel**

Shetland, Eshaness

Johnnie Notions
Hamnavoe
Eshaness
Shetland
ZE2
Tel: 01595 693434
Bod

Shetland, Lerwick

Lerwick Youth Hostel
Islesburgh House
King Harald Street
Lerwick
Shetland
ZE1 0EQ
Tel: 01595 692114
★★★★★ **Hostel**

Shetland, Old Scatness

Betty Mouat's
Old Scatness
Shetland
ZE3 9JW
Tel: 01595 693434
Bod

Shetland, Unst

Gardiesfauld Youth Hostel
Uyeasound
Unst
Shetland
ZE2 9DW
Tel: 01975 755279
★★★ **Hostel**
♿

Shetland, Voe

Sail Loft
Voe
Shetland
ZE2
Tel: 01595 693434
Bod

Shetland, Waas

Voe House
Waas
Shetland
ZE2 9PB
Tel: 01595 693434
Bod

Shetland, Whalsey

Grieve House
Whalsey
Shetland
Tel: 01595 693434
Bod

Shetland, Yell

Windhouse Lodge
Yell
Shetland
Tel: 01595 693434
Bod

Isle of Skye, Ardvasar

Armadale Youth Hostel
Ardvasar
Sleat
Isle of Skye
IV45 8RS
Tel: 01471 844443
★★ **Hostel**

Isle of Skye, Broadford

Broadford Youth Hostel
Broadford
Isle of Skye
IV49 9AA
Tel: 01471 822442
★★★ **Hostel**

Isle of Skye, Kyleakin

Dun Caan Hostel
Pier Road
Kyleakin
Isle of Skye
IV41 8PL
Tel: 01599 534087
★★★★ **Hostel**

Kyleakin Youth Hostel
Kyleakin
Inverness-shire
IV41 8PL
Tel: 0871 330 8535
★★★ **Hostel**

Saucy Mary's Lodge
Kyleakin
IV41 8PL
Tel: 01599 534845
★★★ **Hostel**

Skye Backpackers
Kyleakin
Isle of Skye
IV41 8PH
Tel: 01599 534510
★★ **Backpackers**

Isle of Skye, Portree

Bayfield Backpackers
Bayfield
Portree
Isle of Skye
IV51 9EW
Tel: 01478 612231
★★★★ **Hostel**

Dun Flodigarry Hostel
Flodigarry
Portree
Isle of Skye
IV51 9HZ
Tel: 01470 552212
★★★ **Hostel**

Portree Independent Hostel
Old Post Office
Portree
Isle of Skye
Inverness-shire
IV51 9BT
Tel: 01478 613737
★★★ **Hostel**

Uig Youth Hostel
Portree
Isle of Skye
IV51 9YD
Tel: 0871 330 8556
★★ **Hostel**

Isle of Skye, Sleat

Flora MacDonald Hostel
The Glebe, Kilmore
Sleat
Isle of Skye
IV44 8RG
Tel: 01471 844272
★★★ **Hostel**

Isle of Skye, Sligachan

Sligachan Bunkhouse
Sligachan
Isle of Skye
IV47 8SW
Tel: 01478 650204
★★★ **Hostel**

Spean Bridge

Loch Lochy Youth Hostel
South Laggan
Spean Bridge
Inverness-shire
PH34 4EA
Tel: 0870 0041135
★★ **Hostel**

St Andrews

St Andrews Tourist Hostel
Inchape House
St Mary's Place
St Andrews
Fife
KY16 9UY
Tel: 01334 479911
★★★ **Hostel**

Stirling

Stirling Youth Hostel
St John Street
Stirling
FK8 1EA
Tel: 0871 330 8550
★★★★ **Hostel**
♿

Willy Wallace Hostel
77 Murray Place
Stirling
FK8 1AU
Tel: 01786 446773
★★ **Backpackers**

Strathcarron

Gerry's Achnashellach Hostel
Craig, Achnashellach
Strathcarron
Wester Ross
IV54 8YU
Tel: 01520 766232
★★ **Hostel**

Strathdon

Jenny's Bothy Crofthouse
Corgarff
Strathdon
AB36 8YP
Tel: 01975 651449
★★★ Hostel

Strontian

Ariundle Bunkhouse
Ariundle
Strontian
PH36 4JA
Tel: 01967 402279
★★★★ Hostel
♿

Thurso

Sandra's Backpackers Hostel
24-26 Princes Street
Thurso
Caithness
KW14 7BQ
Tel: 01847 894575
★★★★ Hostel

Isle of Tiree, Cornaigmore

Millhouse Hostel
Cornaigmore
Isle of Tiree
PA77 6XA
Tel: 01879 220435
★★★★ Hostel

Tomintoul

Tomintoul Youth Hostel
Main Street
Tomintoul
Banffshire
AB37 9EX
Tel: 01479 872403
★★★★ Hostel
𝄞𝄞

Tongue, By Lairg

Tongue Youth Hostel
Tongue, By Lairg
Sutherland
IV27 4XH
Tel: 01847 611301
★★★ Hostel
𝄞𝄞

Torridon

Torridon Youth Hostel
Torridon
Ross-shire
IV22 2EZ
Tel: 01445 791284/
0870 0041154
★★★★ Hostel
𝄞𝄞

Tyndrum

By The Way Hostel
Lower Station Road
Tyndrum
FK20 8RY
Tel: 01838 400333
★★★★ Hostel

Ullapool

Achininver Youth Hostel
Achiltibuie
Ross-shire
Ullapool
IV26 2YL
Tel: 01854 613701/
0810 0041100
★★ Hostel
𝄞𝄞

Ullapool Tourist Hostel
West House
West Argyle Street
Ullapool
IV26 2TY
Tel: 01854 613126
★★★★ Hostel

Ullapool Youth Hostel
Shore Street
Ullapool
IV26 2UJ
Tel: 01854 612254
★★★ Hostel
𝄞𝄞𝄞

Weem

Adventurer's Escape
Weem
Aberfeldy
PH15 2LD
Tel: 01887 820498
★★★★ Hostel
𝄞𝄞𝄞

Western Isles, Carloway

Garenin Hostel
Garenin Village
Carloway
West Lewis, Western Isles
HS2 9AL
★ Hostel

No 3 Gearrannan
Gearrannan Blackhouse
Carloway
Isle of Lewis
HS2 9AL
Tel: 01851 643416
★★ Group Accommodation

Western Isles, Drinishader

Drinishader Bunkhouse
Isle of Harris
HS3 3DX
Tel: 01859 511255
★★ Hostel

Western Isles, Harris

**Lewis & Harris
Youth Clubs Association**
Scaladale Centre, Ardvourlie
Western Isles
HS3 3AB
Tel: 01859 502502
★★★★ Activity Accommodation
🧍

Rhenigidale Hostel
Western Isles
HS3 3BD
★ Hostel

Rockview Bunkhouse
Main Street, Tarbert
Western Isles
HS3 3DJ
Tel: 01859 502081
★★ Hostel

Western Isles, Laxdale

Laxdale Bunkhouse
Laxdale Holiday Park
6 Laxdale Lane
Isle of Lewis
HS2 0DP
Tel: 01851 706966
★★★★ Hostel
🧍

Western Isles, Leverburgh

**Am Bothan Leverburgh
Bunkhouse**
Am Bothan
Isle of Harris
HS5 3UA
Tel: 01859 520251
★★★★★ Hostel
♿

Western Isles, Lochmaddy

Uist Outdoor Centre
Isle of Uist
HS6 5AE
Tel: 01876 500480
★★ Hostel

Western Isles, South Galson

Galson Farm
South galston
Isle of Lewis
HS2 0SH
Tel: 01851 850492
★★★★ Hostel

Western Isles, Stornoway

Heb Hostel
25 Kenneth Street
Stornoway
Isle of Lewis
HS1 2DR
Tel: 01851 709889
★★★★ Hostel

nr Wick

John O'Groats Youth Hostel
Canisbay
nr wick
Caithness
KW1 4YH
Tel: 01463 243402 /0870
0041129
★★ Hostel
𝄞𝄞

The following parks provide purpose built toilet and washing facilities for the disabled. However it is recommended that holidaymakers contact parks to ensure that facilities meet their own particular requirements.

The three categories of accessibility, drawn up in close consultation with specialist organisations concerned with the needs of people with disabilities are:

Category 1

Unassisted wheelchair access

Category 2

Assisted wheelchair access

Category 3

Access for visitors with mobility difficulties

Dunbar

Belhaven Bay Caravan Park
Belhaven Bay
Dunbar
East Lothian
EH42 1TU
Tel: 01368 865956
★★★★ Holiday Park
&

**Thurston Manor
Holiday Home Park**
Innerwick
Dunbar
East Lothian
EH42 1SA
Tel: 01368 840643
★★★★★ Holiday Park
&

Edinburgh

Mortonhall Caravan Park
38 Mortonhall Gate
Frogston Road East
Edinburgh
EH16 6TJ
Tel: 0131 664 1533
★★★★ Holiday Park
&

North Berwick

Tantallon Caravan Park
Dunbar Road
North Berwick
East Lothian
EH39 5NJ
Tel: 01620 893348
★★★★ Holiday Park
&

Southerness

Southerness Holiday Village
Southerness
Dumfriesshire
DG2 8AZ
Tel: 01387 880256
★★★★ Holiday Park
&

SOUTH OF SCOTLAND
Ayrshire and Arran, Dumfries and Galloway, Scottish Borders

AYRSHIRE AND ARRAN

Ayr

Craigie Gardens Caravan Club Site
Craigie Road, Ayr, Ayrshire,
KA8 0SS
Tel: 01292 264909
★★★★★ Touring Park

Craig Tara Holiday Park
Dunure Road, Ayr, KA7 4LB
Tel: 01292 265141
★★★★ Holiday Park

Croft Head Caravan Park
by Ayr, KA6 6EN
Tel: 01292 263516
★★★★ Holiday Park

Culzean Bay Holiday Park
Knoweside, By Croyshore,
Maybole, Ayrshire, KA19 8JS
Tel: 01292 500444
★★★★ Holiday Park

Heads of Ayr Caravan Park
Dunure Road, Ayr, Ayrshire,
KA7 4LD
Tel: 01292 442269
★★★★ Holiday Park

Sundrum Castle Holiday Park
by Ayr, KA6 5JH
Tel: 01292 570057
★★★★ Holiday Park

by Ayr

Middlemuir Park
Tarbolton, Nr Ayr, Ayrshire,
KA5 5NR
Tel: 01292 541647
★★★ Holiday Park

Ballantrae

Laggan House Leisure Park
Ballantrae, Ayrshire, KA26 0LL
Tel: 01465 831229
★★★ Holiday Park

Barrhill, by Girvan

Barrhill Holiday Park
Barrhill, nr Girvan, Ayrshire,
KA26 0PZ
Tel: 01465 821355
★★★★ Holiday Park

Queensland Holiday Park
Barrhill, Girvan, Ayrshire,
KA26 0PZ
Tel: 01465 821364
★★★★ Holiday Park

by Girvan

Bennane Shore Holiday Park
Lendalfoot, Ayrshire,
KA26 0JG
Tel: 01465 891233
★★★★★ Holiday Park

Isle of Arran

Kildonan

Sealshore Camp Site
Kildonan, Isle of Arran,
KA27 8SL
Tel: 01770 820320
★★★★ Touring Park

Lamlash

Dyemill House
Lamlash, Isle of Arran,
KA27 8NU
Minimum Standard Holiday
Caravan

Kilwinning

Caravan Holiday Home
Viewfield Manor Holiday
Village, 10 Arran View,
Torranyard, Kilwinning,
Ayrshire, KA13 7RD
Tel: 01698 321769/
07900447702
Awaiting Inspection

**Viewfield Manor Holiday
Village**
Torranard, Kilwinning,
Ayrshire, KA13 7RD
Tel: 01294 850286
★★★★ Holiday Park

Maybole

**Camping & Caravanning
Club Site, Culzean Castle**
Glenside, Culzean Castle,
Culzean, Maybole, Ayrshire,
KA19 8JX
Tel: 01655 760627
★★★★ Touring Park

Croyburnfoot Holiday Park
Croy Shore, Maybole,
Ayrshire, KA19 8JS
Tel: 01292 500239
★★★★ Holiday Park

The Ranch
Culzean Road, by Maybole,
Ayrshire, KA19 8DU
Tel: 01655 882446
★★★★ Holiday Park

**Walled Garden Camping &
Caravan Park**
Kilkerran Estate, Crosshill,
Maybole, Ayrshire, KA19 7SL
Tel: 01655 740323
★★★★ Touring Park

Prestwick

Prestwick Holiday Park
Ayr, Prestwick, Ayrshire,
KA9 1UH
Tel: 01292 479261
★★★ Holiday Park

Saltcoats

Sandylands Holiday Park
Auchenharvie Park, Saltcoats,
Ayrshire, KA21 5JN
Tel: 01294 469411
★★★★ Holiday Park

Turnberry

Turnberry Holiday Park
Turnberry, Girvan, Ayrshire,
KA26 9JW
Tel: 01655 331288
★★★ Holiday Park

DUMFRIES AND GALLOWAY

Annan

**Galabank Caravan &
Camping Site**
North Street, Annan,
Dumfriesshire, DG12 5DQ
Tel: 01461 203539/
01556 503806
★★ Touring Park

**Queensberry Bay
Caravan Park**
Powfoot, Annan,
Dumfriesshire, DG12 5PU
Tel: 01461 700205
★★★★ Holiday Park

Auchenmalg

**Luce Bay Holiday Park &
Lodges**
Auchenmalg, Newton Stewart,
Wigtownshire, DG8 0JT
Tel: 01581 500227
★★★★ Holiday Park

Beattock

Craigielands Country Park
Craigielands Leisure Ltd,
Beattock, Nr Moffat,
Dumfries and Galloway,
DG10 9RE
Tel: 01683 300591
★★★ Holiday Park

Cairnryan

Cairnryan Caravan Park
Cairnryan, Wigtownshire,
DG9 8QX
Tel: 01581 200231
★★★★ Holiday Park

Castle Douglas

Lochside Caravan &
Camping Site
Lochside Park,
by Carlingwark Loch,
Castle Douglas,
Kirkcudbrightshire, DG7 1EZ
Tel: 01556 503806
★★★★ Touring Park

Netheryett Caravan
Netheryett, Castle Douglas,
Kirkcudbrightshire, DG7 3JZ
Tel: 01556 660213
**Minimum Standard Holiday
Caravan**

Creetown

Castle Cary Holiday Park
Crewn, Nr Newton Stewart,
Wigtownshire, DG8 7DQ
Tel: 01671 820264
★★★★ Holiday Park

Creetown Caravan Park
Silver Street, Creetown,
Wigtownshire, DG8 7HU
Tel: 01671 820377
★★★★ Holiday Park

Crocketford, Dumfries

Park of Brandedleys
Crocketford, Dumfries
Tel: 0845 4561760
★★★★ Holiday Park

Dalbeattie

Glenearly Caravan Park
Park Farm, Dalbeattie,
Kirkcudbrightshire, DG5 4NE
Tel: 01556 611393
★★★★ Holiday Park

Sandyhills Bay Leisure Park
Sandyhills, by Dalbeattie,
Kirkcudbrightshire, DG5 4NY
Tel: 01387 780257
★★★★ Holiday Park

Drummore, by Stranraer

Clashwhannon Caravan Park
Drummore, Stranraer,
Wigtown, DG9 9QE
Tel: 01776 840632
★★ Holiday Park

New England Bay Caravan Club Site
Port Logan, Stranraer,
Dumfries & Galloway,
DG9 9NX
Tel: 01776 860275
★★★★ Touring Park

Dumfries

Barnsoul Farm
Shawhead, Dumfries,
DG2 9SQ
Tel: 01387 730249
★★★ Holiday Park

by Dumfries

Beeswing Caravan Park
Drumjohn Moor, Kirkgunzeon,
Kirkcudbrightshire, DG2 8JL
Tel: 01387 760242
★★★★ Holiday Park

Ecclefechan

Cressfield Caravan Park
Ecclefechan, Lockerbie,
Dumfriesshire, DG11 3DR
Tel: 01576 300702/300745
★★★★ Holiday Park

by Ecclefechan

Hoddom Castle Caravan Park
Hoddom, Lockerbie,
Dumfries-shire, DG11 1AS
Tel: 01576 300251
★★★★★ Holiday Park

Gatehouse of Fleet

Anwoth Holiday Park
Gatehouse of Fleet,
Kirkcudbrightshire, DG7 2JU
Tel: 01557 814333
★★★★★ Holiday Park

Mossyard Caravan Park
Mossyard, Gatehouse of Fleet,
Kirkcudbrightshire, DG7 2ET
Tel: 01557 840226
★★★★ Holiday Park

Newton Farm
Gatehouse of Fleet,
Castle Douglas,
Kirkcudbrightshire, DG7 2ER
Tel: 01557 840234
Minimum Standard Holiday Caravan

by Gatehouse of Fleet

Auchenlarie Holiday Park
Gatehouse of Fleet,
Castle Douglas, DG7 2EX
Tel: 01557 840251
★★★★★ Holiday Park

Glenluce

Glenluce Caravan & Camping Park
Glenluce, Wigtownshire,
DG8 0QR
Tel: 01581 300412
★★★★ Holiday Park

Whitecairn Farm Caravan Park
Whitecairn, Glenluce,
Wigtownshire, DG8 0NZ
Tel: 01581 300267
★★★★ Holiday Park

Glentrool, by Bargrennan

Glentrool Holiday Park
Bargrennan, Newton Stewart,
Wigtownshire, DG8 6RN
Tel: 01671 840280
★★★★ Holiday Park

Gretna

Braids Caravan Park
Annan Road, Gretna,
DG16 5DQ
Tel: 01461 337409
★★★ Touring Park

Isle of Whithorn

Burrowhead Holiday Village
Isle of Whithorn,
Newton Stewart,
Wigtownshire, DG8 8JB
Tel: 01988 500252
★★★ Holiday Park

Kippford, by Dalbeattie

Kippford Holiday Park
Kippford,
Kirkcudbrightshire, DG5 4LF
Tel: 01556 620636
★★★★★ Holiday Park

Kirkcudbright

Brighouse Bay Holiday Park
Borgue Road, Kirkcudbright,
Kirkcudbrightshire, DG6 4TS
Tel: 01557 870267
★★★★★ Holiday Park

Seaward Caravan Park
Dhoon Bay, Kirkcudbright,
Kirkcudbrighshire, DG6 4TJ
Tel: 01557 331079
★★★★ Holiday Park

Silvercraigs Caravan & Camping Site
Silvercraigs Road,
Kirkcudbright,
Kirkcudbrightshire, DG6 4BT
Tel: 01556 503806
★★★★ Touring Park

Kirkinner

Drumroamin Farm Camping & Caravan Site
1 South Balfern, Kirkinner,
Newton Stewart, DG8 9DB
Tel: 01988 840613
★★★★ Holiday Park

Kirkpatrick Fleming

King Robert the Bruce's Cave
Cove Estate,
Kirkpatrick Fleming,
Dumfriesshire, DG11 3AT
Tel: 01461 800285
★★★ Holiday Park

Langholm

Ewes Water Caravan & Camping Park
Milntown, Langholm,
Dumfriesshire
Tel: 013873 80386
★★★ Touring Park

Whitshiels Caravan Park
Langholm, Dumfriesshire,
DG13 0HG
Tel: 01387 380494
★★★★ Touring Park

Lochmaben

Kirkloch Caravan & Camping Site
Kirk Loch Brae, Kirk Loch,
Lochmaben, Dumfriesshire
Tel: 01556 503806
★★★ Touring Park

Lockerbie

Halleaths Caravan & Camping Park
Lochmaben, Lockerbie,
Dumfriesshire, DG11 1NA
Tel: 01387 810630
★★★★ Holiday Park

Moffat

Camping & Caravanning Club Site, Moffat
Hammerland's Farm, Moffat,
Dumfriesshire, DG10 9QL
Tel: 01683 220436
★★★★ Touring Park

Newton Stewart

Creebridge Caravan Park
Minnigaff, Newton Stewart,
Wigtownshire, DG8 6AJ
Tel: 01671 402324
★★★ Holiday Park

East Culkae Farmhouse
Sorbie, Newton Stewart,
Wigtownshire, DG8 8AS
Tel: 01988 850214
Minimum Standard Holiday Caravan

by Newton Stewart

Three Lochs Holiday Park
Balminnoch, Newton Stewart,
Wigtownshire, DG8 0EP
Tel: 01671 830304
★★★★ Holiday Park

Palnackie, by Castle Douglas

Barlochan Caravan Park
Palnackie, by Castle Douglas,
Kirkcudbrightshire, DG7 1PF
Tel: 01556 600256
★★★★ Holiday Park

Parton, by Castle Douglas

Loch Ken Holiday Park
Parton, Castle Douglas,
Kirkcudbrightshire, DG7 3NE
Tel: 01644 470282
★★★★ Holiday Park

Penpont, Thornhill

Penpont Caravan Park
Penpont, Thornhill,
Dumfries and Galloway,
DG3 4BQ
Tel: 01848 330470
★★★ Holiday Park

Portpatrick

Castle Bay Caravan Park
Portpatrick, Wigtownshire,
DG9 9AA
Tel: 01776 810462
★★★ Holiday Park

Rockcliffe, by Dalbeattie

Castle Point Caravan Park
Rockcliffe, Rockcliffe,
Galloway, DG5 4QL
Tel: 01556 630248
★★★★ Holiday Park

Sandhead

Sands of Luce Holiday Park
Sandhead, Stranraer,
Wigtownshire, DG9 9JN
Tel: 01776 830456
★★★★ Holiday Park

Southerness

Lighthouse Leisure
Southerness, Dumfriesshire,
DG2 8AZ
Tel: 01387 880277
★★★★ Holiday Park

Southerness Holiday Village
Southerness, Dumfriesshire,
DG2 8AZ
Tel: 01387 880256
★★★★ Holiday Park

Southwick

New Farm
Southwick, Dumfries,
Kirkcudbrightshire, DG2 8AP
Tel: 01387 780285
**Minimum Standard Holiday
Caravan**

Stranraer

Aird Donald Caravan Park
off London Road, Stranraer,
Wigtownshire, DG9 8RN
Tel: 01776 702025
★★★★ Touring Park

by Stranraer

Drumlochart Caravan Park
Lochnaw, Leswalt, Stranraer,
Wigtownshire, DG9 0RN
Tel: 01776 870232
★★★★★ Holiday Park

Wig Bay Holiday Park
Loch Ryan, Stranraer,
Wigtownshire, DG9 0PS
Tel: 01776 853233
★★★★ Holiday Park

by Thornhill

Druidhall Farm
Thornhill, Dumfriesshire,
DG3 4NE
Tel: 01848 600271
**Minimum Standard Holiday
Caravan**

SCOTTISH BORDERS

Cockburnspath

Pease Bay Caravan Park
Cocksburnpath, Berwickshire,
TD13 5YP
Tel: 01368 830206
★★★★★ Holiday Park

Coldingham

Crosslaw Caravan Park
Coldingham, Berwickshire,
TD14 5NS
Tel: 01890 771316
★★★★★ Holiday Park

Scoutscroft Holiday Centre
St Abbs Road, Coldingham,
Berwickshire, TD14 5NB
Tel: 01890 771338 &
01890 771534
★★★★★ Holiday Park

Ettrick Valley

**Honey Cottage Caravan
Park**
Hope House, Ettrick Valley,
Selkirkshire, TD7 5HU
Tel: 01750 62246
★★★ Camping Park

West Deloraine

Ettrick, Selkirkshire, TD7 5HR
**Minimum Standard Holiday
Caravan**

Eyemouth

Eyemouth Holiday Park
Fort Road, Eyemouth,
Berwickshire, TD14 5BE
Tel: 01890 751050
★★★★ Holiday Park

Innerleithen

Tweedside Caravan Park
Montgomery Street,
Innerleithen, Peebleshire,
EH44 6JS
Tel: 01896 831271
★★★ Holiday Park

Jedburgh

**Jedburgh Camping &
Caravanning Club Site**
Elliot Park, Jedburgh,
Roxburghshire, TD8 6EF
Tel: 01835 863393
★★★★ Touring Park

Jedwater Caravan Park
Jedburgh, Roxburghshire,
TD8 6PJ
Tel: 01835 869595
★★★★ Holiday Park

Kelso

Springwood Caravan Park
Springwood Estate, Kelso,
Roxburghshire, TD5 8LS
Tel: 01573 224596
★★★★★ Holiday Park

Lauder

Thirlestane Castle
Caravan and Camping Park,
Lauder, Borders, TD2 6RU
Tel: 01578 718884/
mobile 07976 231032
★★★★ Touring Park

by Lauder

**Lauder Camping &
Caravanning Club Site**
Carfraemill, Oxton, Lauder,
Berwickshire, TD2 6RA
Tel: 01578 750697
★★★★ Touring Park

Melrose

**Gibson Park Caravan Club
Site**
High Street, Melrose,
Roxburghshire, TD6 9RY
Tel: 01896 822969
★★★★★ Touring Park

Peebles

Crossburn Caravan Park
Edinburgh Road, Peebles,
EH45 8ED
Tel: 01721 720501
★★★★ Holiday Park

Selkirk

Victoria Caravan Park
Buccleuch Road, Selkirk,
Selkirkshire, TD7 5DN
Tel: 01750 20897
★★ Touring Park

EDINBURGH AND THE LOTHIANS

EDINBURGH AND LOTHIANS

Aberlady

Aberlady Station Caravan Park
Aberlady, East Lothian,
EH32 0PZ
Tel: 01875 870666
★★★ Touring Park

Blackburn

Mosshall Farm Caravan Park
Blackburn, West Lothian,
EH47 7DB
Tel: 01501 762318
★★ Touring Park

Dalkeith

Lothian Bridge Caravan Park
Newtongrange, Dalkeith,
EH22 4TP
Tel: 0131 663 6120
★★★★ Touring Park

Dirleton

Yellowcraig Caravan Club Site
Dirleton, East Lothian,
EH39 5DS
Tel: 01620 850217
★★★★★ Touring Park

Dunbar

Belhaven Bay Caravan & Camping Park
Belhaven Bay,
Edinburgh Road, Dunbar,
East Lothian
Tel: 01368 865956
★★★★ Holiday Park

C&C Club Site, Barns Ness
Barns Ness, Dunbar,
East Lothian, EH42 1QP
Tel: 01368 863536
★★★ Touring Park

Thurston Manor Holiday Home Park
Innerwick, Dunbar,
East Lothian, EH42 1SA
Tel: 01368 840643
★★★★★ Holiday Park

East Calder

Linwater Caravan Park
West Clifton, East Calder,
EH53 0HT
Tel: 0131 333 3326
★★★★ Touring Park

Edinburgh

Edinburgh Caravan Club Site
Marine Drive, Edinburgh,
EH4 5EN
Tel: 0131 312 6874
★★★★★ Touring Park

Mortonhall Caravan & Camping Park
Frogston Road, Edinburgh,
EH16 6TJ
Tel: 0131 664 1533
★★★★ Holiday Park

Linlithgow

Beecraigs Caravan and Camping Site
Beecraigs Country Park,
Linlithgow, West Lothian
Tel: 01506 844516
★★★★ Touring Park

Longniddry

Seton Sands Caravan Holiday Homes
Seton Sands Holiday Village,
Longniddry, East Lothian,
EH32 0QF
Minimum Standard Holiday Caravan

Seton Sands Holiday Village
Longniddry, East Lothian,
EH32 0QF
Minimum Standard Holiday Caravan

Seton Sands Holiday Village
Longniddry, East Lothian,
EH32 0QF
Tel: 01875 813333
★★★★ Holiday Park

Musselburgh

Drummohr Caravan Park
Levenhall, Musselburgh,
Edinburgh, EH21 8JS
Tel: 0131 665 6867
★★★★★ Touring Park

North Berwick

Gilsland Caravan Park
Grange Road, North Berwick,
East Lothian, EH39 53A
Tel: 01620 892205
★★★ Holiday Park

Tantallon Caravan & Camping Park
Dunbar Road,
North Berwick,
East Lothian, EH39 5NJ
Tel: 01620 893348
★★★★ Holiday Park

GREATER GLASGOW AND CLYDE VALLEY

GREATER GLASGOW AND CLYDE VALLEY

Abington

Mount View Caravan Park
Station Road, Abington,
South Lanarkshire,
ML12 6RW
Tel: 01864 502808
★★★★ Holiday Park

Glasgow

Craigendmuir Park
Craigendmuir Park Business
Centre, Stepps, Glasgow,
G33 6AF
Tel: 0141 779 2973
★★★ Holiday Park

Kilbarchan

Barnbrock Campsite
Clyde Muirshiel Regional Park,
Lochwinnoch, Renfrewshire,
PA10 2PZ
Tel: 01505 614791
★★★ Camping Park

Motherwell

Strathclyde Country Park
Motherwell,
North Lanarkshire, ML1 3ED
Tel: 01698 266155
★★★★ Touring Park

Wemyss Bay

Wemyss Bay Holiday Park
Wemyss Bay, Renfrewshire,
PA18 6BA
Tel: 01475 520812
★★★★ Holiday Park

WEST HIGHLANDS AND ISLANDS, LOCH LOMOND, STIRLING AND TROSSACHS

WEST HIGHLANDS AND ISLANDS

Appin

Appin Holiday Homes
Appin, Argyll, PA38 4BQ
Tel: 01631 730287
★★★★ Holiday Park

Benderloch, by Oban

Tralee Bay Purple Thistle Holidays
Benderloch, by Oban, Argyll, PA37 1QR
Tel: 01631 720255
★★★★★ Holiday Park

Campbeltown

Seaviews at Pennyseorach Farm
Southend, By Campbeltown, Argyll, PA28 6RF
Tel: 01586 830217
Minimum Standard Holiday Caravan

Carradale

Carradale Bay Caravan Park
Carradale, Kintyre, Argyll, PA28 6QG
Tel: 01583 431665
★★★★ Holiday Park

Connel

Camping & Caravanning Club Site, Oban
Barcaldine, Connel, Arygll, PA37 1SG
Tel: 01631 720348
★★★★ Touring Park

Cluaran House
Ardconnel Farm, Connel, Argyll, PA37 1RN
Tel: 01631 710051
Minimum Standard Holiday Caravan

Cruachan View
Ardconnel Farm, Connel, Argyll, PA37 1RN
Tel: 01631 710750
Minimum Standard Holiday Caravan

Dunoon

Hunters Quay Holiday Village
Hunters Quay, Dunoon, Argyll, PA23 8HP
Tel: 01369 707772
★★★★★ Holiday Park

Ford, by Lochgilphead

Stroneskar Farm
Ford, by Lochgilphead, Argyll, PA31 8RJ
Tel: 01546 810286
Minimum Standard Holiday Caravan

Glendaruel

Glendaruel Caravan Park
Glendaruel, Argyll, PA22 3AB
Tel: 01369 820267
★★★★★ Holiday Park

Inveraray

Argyll Caravan Park
Inveraray, Argyll, PA32 8XT
Tel: 01499 302285
★★★★★ Holiday Park

Isle of Bute

Rothesay

Roseland Caravan Park
Canada Hill, Rothesay, Isle of Bute, PA20 9EH
Tel: 01700 504529
★★★★ Holiday Park

Isle of Islay

Lagavulin, by Port Ellen

Tigh na Suil
Lagavulin, Port Ellen, Isle of Islay, Argyll, PA42 7DX
Tel: 01496 302483
Minimum Standard Holiday Caravan

Isle of Mull

Aros

Crannich Farm
Aros, Isle of Mull, PA72 6JP
Tel: 01680 300495
Minimum Standard Holiday Caravan

Bunessan

Newcrofts
6 Uisken Road, Bunessan, Isle of Mull, PA67 6PS
Tel: 01681 700471/ 07787 743369
Minimum Standard Holiday Caravan

Craignure

David & Moira Gracie
Shieling Holidays,
Craignure, Isle of Mull
Tel: 01680 812496
★★★★★ Camping Park

Inverlussa
by Craignure, Isle of Mull, PA65 6BD
Tel: 01680 812436
Minimum Standard Holiday Caravan

Fishnish

Balmeanach Park
Balmeanach, Fishnish, Isle of Mull, Argyll, PA65 6BA
Tel: 01680 300342
★★★★ Touring Park

Salen, Aros

Pennygown Farm
Isle of Mull, PA72 6JN
Tel: 01680 300335
Minimum Standard Holiday Caravan

Rock Cottage
Aros, Isle of Mull, Argyll, PA72 6JB
Tel: 01680 300506
Minimum Standard Holiday Caravan

Tobermory

Lochnameal
by Tobermory, Isle of Mull, Argyll, PA75 6QB
Tel: 01688 302364
Minimum Standard Holiday Caravan

Tobermory Campsite
Newdale, Dervaig Road, Tobermory, Isle of Mull, PA75 6QF
Tel: 01688 302624/302525
★★★ Camping Park

Kilberry, by Tarbert

Port Ban Holiday Park Ltd
Kilberry, Tarbert, Argyll, PA29 6YD
Tel: 01880 770224
★★★ Holiday Park

Kilchrenan

Mrs J MacDougall,
Cuilreoch Kilchrenan,
Taynuilt, Argyll, PA35 1HG
Tel: 01866 833236
Minimum Standard Holiday
Caravan

Kilmun, by Dunoon

Seaforth Cottage
Kilmun, Argyll, PA23 8SE
Tel: 01369 840008
Minimum Standard Holiday Caravan

Lochgoilhead

Drimsynie & Kingfisher Holiday Village
Drimsynie Estate, Lochgoilhead, Argyll, PA24 8AD
Tel: 01301 703312
★★★★ Holiday Park

Isle of Luing

Sunnybrae
South Cuan, Island of Luing, by Oban, Argyll, PA34 4TU
Tel: 01852 314274
★★★★ Holiday Park

Machrihanish

Machrihanish Caravan & Camping Park
East Trodigal, Machrihanish, Campbeltown, Argyll, PA28 6PT
Tel: 01586 810366
★★★★ Touring Park

Oban

An Tobar
Lerags, Oban, Argyll, PA34 4SE
Tel: 01631 565081
Minimum Standard Holiday Caravan

North Ledaig Caravan Club Site
Connel, Oban, Argyll, PA37 1RU
Tel: 01631 710291
★★★★★ Touring Park

Oban continued

Oban
Caravan & Camping Park
Gallanachmore Farm,
Gallanach Road, Oban, Argyll,
PA34 4QH
Tel: 01631 562425
★★★ Holiday Park

Oban Divers Caravan Park
Glenshellach Road, Oban,
Argyll, PA34 4QJ
Tel: 01631 562755
★★★★ Touring Park

Teanga-Bhuidhe
Glencruitten, Oban, PA34 4QA
Minimum Standard Holiday Caravan

Peninver, by Campbeltown

Peninver Sands Holiday Park
Craig View, Peninver,
by Campbeltown, Argyll,
PA28 6QP
Tel: 01586 552262
★★★★ Holiday Park

Peniver Beach
by Campbeltown, Argyll,
PA28 6PW
Minimum Standard Holiday Caravan

Tayinloan, by Tarbert

Point Sands
Tayinloan, by Tarbert, Argyll,
PA29 6XG
Tel: 01583 441263
★★★ Holiday Park

Taynuilt

Curacao Holiday Caravan
Curacao, Taynuilt, Argyll,
PA35 1HW
Tel: 01866 822636
Minimum Standard Holiday Caravan

LOCH LOMOND AND THE TROSSACHS

by Aberfoyle

Cobleland Campsite
Gartmore, by Aberfoyle,
Perthshire, FK8 3UX
Tel: 01877 382392
★★ Touring Park

by Ardlui

Beinglas Farm Campsite
Inverarnan, Ardlui,
Dumbartonshire, G83 7DX
Tel: 01301 704281
★★★★ Camping Park

Arrochar

Ardgarten Camping & Caravanning Club Site
Coilessan Road, Arrochar,
Dunbartonshire, G83 7AR
Tel: 01301 702253
★★★ Touring Park

Ardgarten Campsite
Arrochar, Dunbartonshire,
G83 7AR
Tel: 01301 702293
★★★ Touring Park

Balloch

Lomond Woods Holiday Park
Balloch, Loch Lomond,
G83 8QP
Tel: 01389 755000
★★★★★ Holiday Park

Balmaha

Camping & Caravanning Club Site, Milarochy Bay
Balmaha, Drymen, Glasgow,
G63 0AL
Tel: 01360 870236
★★★★ Touring Park

Callander

Gart Caravan Park
Stirling Road, Callander,
Perthshire, FK17 8LE
Tel: 01877 330002
★★★★★ Holiday Park

Keltie Bridge Caravan Park
Callander, Perthshire, FK17 8LQ
Tel: 01877 330606
★★★★ Touring Park

by Crianlarich

Glendochart Caravan Park
Luib, Crianlarich, Perthshire,
FK20 8QT
Tel: 01567 820637
★★★★ Holiday Park

Drymen

Drymen Camping
Easter Drumquhassle Farm,
Gartness Road, Drymen,
Stirlingshire, G63 0DN
Tel: 01360 660597
★★ Camping Park

Inverbeg

Inverbeg Holiday Park
Inverbeg, by Luss,
Dunbartonshire, G83 8PD
Tel: 01436 860267
★★★★ Holiday Park

Inveruglas

Loch Lomond Holiday Park
Inveruglas, Tarbet,
Argyll & Bute, G83 7DW
Tel: 01301 704224
★★★★★ Holiday Park

Luss

Camping & Caravanning Club Site, Luss
Luss Camping Ground,
Loch Lomond, Alexandria,
G83 8NT
Tel: 01436 860658
★★★★ Touring Park

Rosneath

Rosneath Castle Caravan Park Ltd
Rosneath, by Helensburgh,
Argyll & Bute, G84 0QS
Tel: 01436 831208/831391
★★★★★ Holiday Park

Rowardennan

Cashel Campsite
Rowardennan, by Balmaha,
Stirlingshire, G63 0AW
Tel: 01360 870234
★★★★ Touring Park

Strathyre

Immervoulin Caravan & Camping Park
Strathyre, Perthshire,
FK18 8NJ
Tel: 01877 384285/384682
★★★ Touring Park

Trossachs, by Callander

Trossachs Holiday Park
Gartmore, Stirling, FK8 3SA
Tel: 01877 382614
★★★★★ Holiday Park

Tyndrum, by Crianlarich

Strathfillan Wigwams
Auchtertyre, Tyndrum,
Perthshire, FK20 8RU
Tel: 01838 400251
★★★ Camping Park

STIRLING AND FORTH VALLEY

Fintry

Balgair Castle Caravan Park
Overglinns, Fintry,
Stirlingshire, G63 0LP
Tel: 01360 860283
★★★★ Holiday Park

Gargunnock

Redhall Farm
Gargunnock, Stirlingshire,
FK8 3AE
Tel: 01786 860204
Minimum Standard Holiday Caravan

Killin

Cruachan Farm Caravan & Camping Park
Cruachan, Killin, Perthshire,
FK21 8TY
Tel: 01567 820302
★★★ Holiday Park

Maragowan Caravan Club Site
Aberfeldy Road, Killin, Stirling,
FK21 8TN
Tel: 01567 820245
★★★★★ Touring Park

Lochearnhead

Balquhidder Braes Caravan Park
Balquhidder Station,
Lochearnhead, Perthshire,
FK19 8NX
Tel: 01567 830293
★★★★ Holiday Park

Stirling

Auchenbowie Caravan Site
Auchenbowie, by Stirling,
Stirlingshire, FK6 6RF
Tel: 01324 822141
★★★ Holiday Park

West Drip Farm
Stirling, FK9 4UJ
Minimum Standard Holiday Caravan

Witches Craig Caravan Park
Blairlogie, Stirling, FK9 5PX
Tel: 01786 474947
★★★★★ Touring Park

PERTHSHIRE, ANGUS AND DUNDEE AND THE KINGDOM OF FIFE

PERTHSHIRE

Aberfeldy

Aberfeldy Caravan Park
Dunkeld Road, Aberfeldy,
Perthshire, PH15 2AQ
Tel: 01887 820662
★★★★ Touring Park

Auchterarder

Auchterarder Caravan Park
Nether Coul, Auchterarder,
Perthshire, PH3 1ET
Tel: 01764 663119
★★★★ Touring Park

Blair Atholl

Blair Castle Caravan Park
Blair Atholl, Perthshire,
PH18 5SR
Tel: 01796 481263
★★★★★ Holiday Park

Blairgowrie

Blairgowrie Holiday Park
Blairgowrie, Perthshire,
PH10 7AL
Tel: 01250 876666
★★★★★ Holiday Park

Five Roads Caravan Park
by Alyth, Blairgowrie,
Perthshire, PH11 8NB
Tel: 01828 632255
★★★★ Holiday Park

Bridge of Cally

Corriefodly Holiday Park
Bridge of Cally, PH10 7JG
Tel: 01250 876666
★★★★★ Holiday Park

Cargill, by Perth

Beech Hedge Caravan Park
Cargill, Perth, Perthshire,
PH2 6DU
Tel: 01250 883249
★★★ Holiday Park

Comrie

West Lodge Caravan Park
Comrie, Perthshire, PH6 2LS
Tel: 01764 670354
★★★★ Holiday Park

Crieff

Braidhaugh Park
South Bridgend, Crieff,
Perthshire, PH7 4DH
Tel: 01764 652951
★★★★ Holiday Park

Dunkeld

Erigmore House Holiday Park
Birnam, Dunkeld, Perthshire,
PH8 0BJ
Tel: 01350 727236
★★★★ Holiday Park

by Dunkeld

Invermill Farm Caravan Park
Inver, Dunkeld, Perthshire,
PH8 0JR
Tel: 01350 727477
★★★★ Touring Park

Kinross

Gallowhill Farm Camping and Caravan Park
Gallowhill Farm, Kinross,
Kinross-shire, KY13 0RD
Tel: 01577 862364
★★★ Touring Park

Pitlochry

Faskally Caravan Park
Faskally, Pitlochry, Perthshire,
PH16 5LA
Tel: 01796 472007
★★★★ Holiday Park

Glengoulandie Country Park
By Pitlochry, Perthshire,
PH16 5NL
Tel: 01887 830495
★★★ Holiday Park

Milton of Fonab Caravan Site
Bridge Road, Pitlochry,
Perthshire, PH16 5NA
Tel: 01796 472882
★★★★ Holiday Park

Scone, by Perth

Camping & Caravanning Club Site, Scone
Scone Palace, Scone, Perth,
Perthshire, PH2 6BB
Tel: 01738 552323
★★★★ Touring Park

Crieff

Tummel Bridge

Tummel Valley Holiday Park
Nr Pitlochry, Perthshire,
PH16 5SA
Tel: 01882 634221
★★★★ Holiday Park

ANGUS AND DUNDEE

Carnoustie

Woodlands Caravan Park
Newton Road, Carnoustie,
Angus, DD7 7SR
Tel: 01241 854430
★★★★ Touring Park

Edzell

Glenesk Caravan Park
by Edzell, Brechin, Angus,
DD9 7YP
Tel: 01356 648565
★★★★ Holiday Park

Forfar

Foresterseat Caravan Park
Burnside, Arbroath Road,
Forfar, DD8 2RY
Tel: 01307 818880
★★★★ Touring Park

Leckaway Caravan
South Leckaway Farm,
By Forfar, Angus, DD8 1XF
Tel: 01307 463324
Minimum Standard Holiday Caravan

Lochlands Caravan Park
Lochlands, Dundee Road,
Forfar, Angus, DD8 1XF
Tel: 01307 463621
★★★ Touring Park

Lochside Caravan Park
Forfar Country Park,
Craig O' Loch Road, Forfar,
Angus, DD8 1BT
Tel: 01307 468917/464201
★★★★ Touring Park

Glenisla

Nether Craig Caravan Park
by Alyth, Blairgowrie,
Perthshire, PH11 8HN
Tel: 01575 560204
★★★★★ Touring Park

Monifieth, by Dundee

Riverview Caravan Park
Marine Drive, Monifieth,
By Dundee, Angus, DD5 4NN
Tel: 01382 817979
★★★★★ Holiday Park

Montrose

South Links Caravan Park
Traill Drive, Montrose, Angus,
DD10 8AJ
Tel: 01674 672105
(office hours)
★★★★ Touring Park

Roundyhill, by Glamis

Drumshademuir Caravan Park
Roundyhill, by Glamis, Angus,
DD8 1QT
Tel: 01575 573284
★★★★★ Holiday Park

FIFE

Crail

Sauchope Links Park
Crail, Fife, KY10 3XJ
Tel: 01333 450460
★★★★★ Holiday Park

Elie

Shell Bay Caravan
Shell Bay Caravan Park,
Near Elie, East Neuk of Fife,
Fife, KY9 1HB
Tel: 07779330746
Minimum Standard Holiday Caravan

Glenrothes

Kingdom Caravan Park
1 Overstenton Farm,
Glenrothes, Fife, KY6 2NG
Tel: 01592 772226
★★★★★ Holiday Park

Letham Feus, by Leven

Letham Feus Caravan Park
Cupar Road,
By Lundin Links, Fife,
KY8 4NT
Tel: 01333 351900
★★★★ Holiday Park

Lundin Links

Woodland Gardens Caravan & Camping Park
Blindwell Road, Lundin Links, Fife, KY8 5QG
Tel: 01333 360319
★★★★ Holiday Park

Markinch

Balbirnie Park Caravan Club Site
Balbirnie Road, Markinch, Glenrothes, Fife, KY7 6NR
Tel: 01592 759130
★★★★ Touring Park

Pittenweem

Grangemuir Woodland Caravan Park
Grangemuir, Pittenweem, Fife, KY10 2RB
Tel: 01333 311213
★★★★ Touring Park

St Andrews

Cairnsmill Caravan Park
Largo Road, St Andrews, Fife, KY16 8NN
Tel: 01334 473604
★★★★ Holiday Park

Caravan C4
Kinell Braes Caravan Park, St Andrews, Fife, KY16 8PX
Tel: 01698 816935
Minimum Standard Holiday Caravan

Clayton Caravan Park
St Andrews, Fife, KY16 9YB
Tel: 01334 870242
★★★★ Holiday Park

Craigtoun Meadows Holiday Park
Mount Melville, St Andrews, Fife, KY16 8PQ
Tel: 01334 475959
★★★★★ Holiday Park

G2
Kinkell Braes Caravan Park, St Andrews, Fife, KY16 8PX
Minimum Standard Holiday Caravan

Kinkell Braes Caravan Park
St Andrews, Fife, KY16 8PX
Tel: 01334 474250
Minimum Standard Holiday Caravan

Knockhill of Nydie
St Andrews, Fife, KY16 9SL
Tel: 01334 850110
Awaiting Inspection

Upper Largo

Monturpie Caravan Park
Monturpie, Upper Largo, Leven, Fife, KY8 5QS
Tel: 01333 360254
★★★ Touring Park

ABERDEEN AND GRAMPIAN HIGHLANDS:
Scotland's Castle and Whisky Country

ABERDEEN AND GRAMPIAN

Aberdeen

Lower Deeside Holiday Park
Maryculter, Aberdeen, AB12 5FX
Tel: 01224 733860
★★★★ Holiday Park

by Aberlour

Aberlour Gardens
Caravan & Camping Park, Aberlour-on-Spey, Morayshire, AB38 9LD
Tel: 01340 871586
★★★★★ Holiday Park

Aboyne

Royal Deeside Log Cabins
By Loch Kinord, Dinnet, Aboyne, Royal Deeside, Aberdeenshire, AB34 5LW
Tel: 013398 85229
Minimum Standard Holiday Caravan

Waterside
Birse, Aboyne, AB34 5BU
Awaiting Inspection

Alford

Haughton Caravan Park
Montgarrie Road, Alford, Aberdeenshire, AB33 8NA
Tel: 01975 562107
★★★★ Holiday Park

Ballater

Ballater Caravan Park
Anderson Road, Ballater, Kincardineshire, AB35 5QR
Tel: 01339 855727
★★★ Holiday Park

Banchory

Feughside Caravan Park
Strachan, Banchory, Aberdeenshire, AB31 6NT
Tel: 01330 850669
★★★★ Holiday Park

Banff

Banff Links Caravan Park
Banff Links, Banff, Grampian, AB45 2JJ
Tel: 01261 812228
★★★★ Holiday Park

Myrus Holiday Park
Myrus Crossroads, Macduff, By Banff, AB45 3QP
Tel: 01261 812228
★★★★★ Holiday Park

Braemar

The Invercauld Caravan Club Site
Glenshee Road, Braemar, Ballater, Aberdeenshire, AB35 5YQ
Tel: 01339 741373
★★★★ Touring Park

Buckie

Strathlene Caravan Park
Portessie, Buckie, Banffshire, AB56 1SR
Tel: 01542 834851
★★★★ Holiday Park

Catterline

Cloak Caravan Park
Catterline, By Stonehaven, AB39
Tel: 01569 750232
Minimum Standard Holiday Caravan

by Craigellachie

Camping & Caravanning Club Site, Speyside
Archiestown, Aberlour, Morayshire, AB38 9SL
Tel: 01340 810414
★★★★ Touring Park

Cruden Bay

Craighead Caravan Park
Cruden Bay, Peterhead, Aberdeenshire, AB42 0PL
Tel: 01779 812251
★★★ Holiday Park

Cullen

Cullen Bay Holiday Park
Cullen, Banffshire, AB56 4TW
Tel: 01542 840766
★★★★ Holiday Park

Elgin

Station Caravan Park
West Beach, Hopeman, Elgin, Morayshire, IV30 5RU
Tel: 01343 830880
★★★★ Holiday Park

Findhorn

Findhorn Bay Caravan Park
Findhorn, by Forres, Morayshire, IV36 3TY
Tel: 01309 690203
★★★ Holiday Park

Findhorn Sands Caravan Park
Findhorn, Forres, Morayshire, IV36 0YZ
Tel: 01309 690324
★★★★★ Holiday Park

Fordoun

Brownmuir Caravan Park
Fordoun, Laurencekirk,
Aberdeenshire, AB30 1SJ
Tel: 01561 320786
★★★ Holiday Park

Fraserburgh

Esplanade Caravan Park
Harbour Road, Fraserburgh,
Aberdeenshire, AB43 5EU
Tel: 01346 510041
★★★ Holiday Park

Huntly

Huntly Castle Caravan Park
The Meadows, Huntly,
Aberdeenshire, AB54 4UJ
Tel: 01466 794999
★★★★★ Holiday Park

Inverbervie

Inverbervie Caravan Park
Kirkburn, Inverbervie, Angus,
DD10 0SP
Tel: 07791 678997
★★★ Holiday Park

Johnshaven

Wairds Park Caravan Park
Beach Road, Johnshaven,
Kincardineshire, DD10 0HD
Tel: 01561 362395
★★★★ Holiday Park

Kintore

Hillhead Caravan Park
Kintore, Aberdeenshire,
AB51 0YX
Tel: 01467 632809
★★★★ Holiday Park

Laurencekirk

Dovecot Caravan Park
Northwater Bridge,
by Laurencekirk, AB30 1QL
Tel: 01674 840630
★★★ Holiday Park

Lossiemouth

Silver Sands Leisure Park
Covesea, West Beach,
Lossiemouth, Morayshire,
IV31 6SP
Tel: 01343 813262
★★★★ Holiday Park

by Macduff

**Wester Bonnyton Farm
Caravan Site**
Gamrie, by MacDuff,
Banffshire, AB45 3EP
Tel: 01261 832470
★★★ Holiday Park

Mintlaw

Aden Caravan Park
Aden Country Park, Mintlaw,
Grampian, Aberdeenshire,
AB42 8FQ
Tel: 01771 623460
★★★★★ Holiday Park

Peterhead

**Peterhead Lido Caravan
Park**
The Lido, Peterhead,
Grampian, AB42 2YP
Tel: 01779 473358
★★★★ Holiday Park

Portsoy

Portsoy Caravan Park
The Links, Portsoy, Grampian,
AB45 2RQ
Tel: 01261 842695
★★★★ Holiday Park

Rosehearty, by Fraserburgh

Rosehearty Caravan Park
The Harbour, Rosehearty,
Grampian, AB43 7JQ
Tel: 01346 561314
★★ Touring Park

St Cyrus

East Bowstrips Caravan
Park
St Cyrus, Nr Montrose,
Aberdeenshire, DD10 0DE
Tel: 01674 850328
★★★★★ Holiday Park

Sandend, by Portsoy

Sandend Caravan Park
Sandend, by Portsoy,
Banffshire, AB4 2UA
Tel: 01261 842660
★★★★ Holiday Park

Stonehaven

**Queen Elizabeth Caravan
Park**
Cowie, Stonehaven,
Kincardineshire, AB39 2RP
Tel: 01569 764041
★★★ Holiday Park

Tarland

**Tarland Camping &
Caravanning Club Site**
Drummie Hill, Tarland,
Aboyne, Aberdeenshire,
AB34 4UP
Tel: 01339 881388/
0870 2433331
★★★★★ Touring Park

Turriff

Turriff Caravan Park
Station Road, Turriff,
Grampian, AB53 7ER
Tel: 01888 562205
★★★★ Holiday Park

THE HIGHLANDS AND SKYE

NORTHERN HIGHLANDS, INVERNESS, LOCH NESS AND NAIRN

Armadale

Poulouriscaig
169 West End, Armadale,
Caithness, KW14 7SA
Minimum Standard Holiday
Caravan

Aultbea

Burnside
48 Mellon Charles, Aultbea,
Ross-shire, IV22 2JL
Minimum Standard Holiday
Caravan

30 Mellon Charles
Aultbea, by Achnasheen,
Ross-shire, IV22 2JN
Tel: 01445 731499
Minimum Standard Holiday
Caravan

Sea Croft
51 Mellon Charles, Aultbea,
Ross-shire, IV22 2JL
Tel: 01445 731367
Minimum Standard Holiday
Caravan

Balmacara

Reraig Caravan Site
Balmacara,
Kyle of Lochalsh,
Ross-shire, IV40 8DH
Tel: 01599 566215
★★★★ Touring Park

Beauly

Rheindown Farm
Beauly, Inverness-shire,
IV4 7AB
Tel: 01463 782461
Minimum Standard Holiday
Caravan

Bettyhill

99 Kirtomy
Bettyhill, Nr Thurso,
Sutherland, KW14 7TB
Tel: 01641 521253
Minimum Standard Holiday
Caravan

Brora

Dalchalm Caravan Club Site
Dalchalm, Brora, Sutherland,
KW9 6LP
Tel: 01408 621479
★★★★★ Touring Park

Cannich

Cannich Caravan &
Camping Park
Cannich, By Beauly,
Inverness-shire, IV4 7LN
Tel: 01456 415364
★★★★ Holiday Park

Contin

Riverside Chalets & Caravan
Park
Contin, Ross-shire, IV14 9ES
Tel: 0800 074 4843
★★ Touring Park

Culloden Moor

Culloden Moor Caravan Club
Site
Newlands, Culloden Moor,
Inverness-shire, IV2 5EF
Tel: 01463 790625
★★★★★ Touring Park

Dingwall

Camping & Caravanning
Club Site, Dingwall
Jubilee Park Road, Dingwall,
Ross-shire, IV15 9QZ
Tel: 01349 862236
★★★★ Touring Park

Dornoch

Dornoch Links Caravan
Park
Dornoch, IV25 3LQ
Minimum Standard Holiday
Caravan

Dornoch Caravan Park
The Links, River Street,
Dornoch, Sutherland,
IV25 3LX
Tel: 01862 810423
★★★★ Holiday Park

Pitgrudy Caravan Park
Poles Road, Dornoch,
Sutherland, IV25 3HY
Tel: 01862 821253/810001
★★★★ Holiday Park

Seaview Farm Caravan Park
Seaview, Hilton, Dornoch,
Sutherland, IV25 3PW
Tel: 01862 810294
★★ Touring Park

Dunbeath

Inver Caravan Park
Houstry Road, Dunbeath,
Caithness, KW6 6EH
Tel: 01593 731441
★★★ Touring
Park

Dundonnell

4 Camusnagaul
Dundonnell, IV23 2QT
Minimum Standard Holiday
Caravan

Badrallach DB&B, Bothy,
Cottage & Camp Site
Croft No 9, Badrallach,
Dundonnell, Ross-shire
Tel: 01854 633281
★★★★ Camping Park

Dunnet

Dunnet Bay Caravan Club
Site
Dunnet, Thurso, KW14 8XD
Tel: 01847 821319
★★★★★ Touring Park

Embo, by Dornoch

Grannies Heilan Hame
Holiday Park
Embo, Dornoch, Sutherland,
IV25 3QD
Tel: 01862 810383
★★★★ Holiday Park

Evanton

Black Rock Caravan Park
Balconie Street, Evanton,
Ross-shire, IV16 9UN
Tel: 01349 830917
★★★★★ Holiday Park

Fort Augustus

Fort Augustus Caravan and
Camping Park
Market Hill, Fort Augustus,
Inverness-shire, PH32 4DS
Tel: 01320 366618
★★★★ Touring Park

Gairloch

Gairloch Caravan &
Camping Park
Strath, Gairloch, Ross-shire,
IV21 2BX
Tel: 01445 712373
★★★★ Touring Park

Sands Holiday Centre
Gairloch, Ross-shire,
IV21 2DL
Tel: 01445 712152
★★★★ Holiday Park

Invergarry

Faichemard Farm Camping
Site
Faichemard Farm, Invergarry,
Inverness-shire, PH35 4HG
Tel: 01809 501314
★★★★ Touring Park

Invermoriston

Loch Ness Caravan &
Camping Park
Invermoriston,
Inverness-shire, IV63 7YE
Tel: 01320 351207/351399
★★★★★ Touring Park

Inverness

Auchnahillin Caravan &
Camping Park
Daviot East,
Inverness-shire, IV2 5XQ
Tel: 01463 772286
★★★★ Holiday Park

Bught Caravan Park
Bught Park, Bught Lane,
Inverness, Inverness-shire,
IV3 5SR
Tel: 01463 236920
★★★ Holiday Park

High Country Holidays
Leachkin, Inverness, IV3 8PW
Tel: 01463 241831
Minimum Standard Holiday
Caravan

The Croft
9 Leachkin, Inverness,
Inverness-shire, IV3 8PN
Minimum Standard Holiday
Caravan

John o'Groats

John O'Groats Caravan Site
John O'Groats, Caithness,
KW1 4YR
Tel: 01955 611329
★★★ Touring Park

Kinlochewe

Kinlochewe Caravan Club
Site
Kinlochewe, Achnasheen,
Highland, IV22 2PA
Tel: 01445 760239
★★★★ Touring Park

Laide

The Sheiling
Achgarve, Laide, Ross-shire,
IV22 2NS
Tel: 01445 731487
Minimum Standard Holiday
Caravan

Lairg

Dunroamin Caravan Park
Main Street, Lairg, Sutherland,
IV27 4AR
Tel: 01549 402447
★★★★ Touring Park

Melvich

Halladale Inn Caravan Park
Melvich, Sutherland,
KW14 7YJ
Tel: 01641 531282
★★★★ Touring Park

Nairn

Camping & Caravanning
Club Site,Nairn
Delnies Woods, Nairn,
Nairnshire, IV12 5NX
Tel: 01667 455281
★★★★ Touring Park

Nairn Lochloy Holiday Park
East Beach, Nairn, Nairnshire,
IV12 4PH
Tel: 01667 453764
★★★★ Holiday Park

Plot 130
Nairn Lochloy Holiday Park,
Nairn, Inverness-shire,
IV12 4PH
Tel: 01463 790953
Minimum Standard Holiday
Caravan

by Nairn

Laikenbuie
Grantown Road, Nairn,
IV12 5QN
Tel: 01667 454630
Minimum Standard Holiday
Caravan

Oldshoremore

142 Oldshoremore
Rhiconich, By Lairg,
IV27
Tel: 01971 521335
Minimum Standard Holiday
Caravan

Poolewe

Gardens Camping &
Caravanning Club Site
Inverewe Gardens, Poolewe,
Ross-shire, IV22 2LF
Tel: 01445 781249
★★★★ Touring Park

Rosemarkie

Camping & Caravanning
Club Site, Rosemarkie
Ness Road East, Fortrose,
Fortrose, Ross-shire, IV10 8SE
Tel: 01381 621117
★★★★ Touring Park

by Tain

Dornoch Firth Caravan Park
Meikle Ferry South, by Tain,
Ross-shire, IV19 1JX
Tel: 01862 892292
★★★★ Holiday Park

Thurso

Scrabster Caravan Park
Thurso, Caithness, KW14 8BN
Minimum Standard Holiday
Caravan

Thurso Caravan & Camping
Park
Smith Terrace,
Scrabster Road, Thurso,
Caithness, KW14 7JY
Tel: 01847 894631
★★★ Holiday Park

Ullapool

Ardmair Point Holiday Park
Ardmair Point, Ullapool,
Ross-shire, IV26 2TN
Tel: 01854 612054
★★★★ Touring Park

Wick

Wick Caravan & Camping
Park
Riverside Drive, Janetstown,
Wick, Caithness, KW1 4RG
Tel: 01955 605420
★★★★ Touring Park

FORT WILLIAM AND LOCHABER, SKYE AND LOCHALSH

Acharacle

Burnbank
Acharacle, Argyll, PH36 4JL
Tel: 01967 431223
Minimum Standard Holiday
Caravan

Achateny

Branault
Achateny, Acharacle, Argyll,
PH36 4LG
Tel: 01972 510284
Minimum Standard Holiday
Caravan

Ardelve, by Dornie

Ardelve
Dornie, Kyle of Lochalsh,
Ross-shire, IV40 8DY
Minimum Standard Holiday
Caravan

Ardnamurchan

Resipole Farm Caravan Park
Loch Sunart, by Acharacle,
Argyll, PH36 4HX
Tel: 01967 431235
★★★★ Holiday Park

Arisaig

Camusdarach
Camusdarach Lodge, Arisaig,
Inverness-shire, PH39 4NT
Tel: 01687 450221
★★★★ Touring Park

Gorten Sands Caravan Site
Gorten Farm, Arisaig,
Inverness-shire, PH39 4NS
Tel: 01687 450283
★★★★ Touring Park

Kinloid Cottages & Caravans
Kinloid, Arisaig, PH39 4NS
Tel: 01687 450366
Minimum Standard Holiday
Caravan

Ballachulish

The Camping and
Caravanning Clubsite
Glencoe
Ballachulish, Argyll, PH49 4LA
Tel: 01855 811397
★★★★ Touring Park

Corpach, by Fort William

Cruachan
19 Badabrie, Corpach,
Fort William, PH33 7JB
Tel: 01397 772573
Minimum Standard Holiday
Caravan

Fort William

Glen Nevis Holiday
Caravans
Glen Nevis, Fort William,
PH33 6SX
Tel: 01397 702191
★★★★★ Holiday Park

Linnhe Lochside Holidays
Corpach, Fort William,
Inverness-shire, PH33 7NL
Tel: 01397 772376
★★★★★ Holiday Park

Lochy Caravan Park
Camaghael, Fort William,
Inverness-shire, PH33 7NF
Tel: 01397 703446
★★★★ Holiday Park

Glencoe

Invercoe Caravan Camping
Park
Glencoe, Argyll, PH49 4HP
Tel: 01855 811210
★★★★★ Holiday Park

Red Squirrel Camp Site
Leacantuim Farm, Glencoe,
Argyll, PA49 4HX
Tel: 01855 811256
★★ Camping Park

Inverinate, by Kyle of Lochalsh

Morvich Caravan Club Site
Shiel Bridge, Ross-shire
IV40 8HQ
Tel: 01599 511354
★★★★★ Touring Park

Isle of Skye

Dunvegan

Kinloch Campsite
Dunvegan, Isle of Skye,
IV55 8GU
Tel: 01470 521210
★★★ Touring Park

159

Portree

Torvaig Caravan & Camping Park
8 Torvaig, Portree,
Isle of Skye, IV51 9HU
Tel: 01478 611849
★★★ Touring Park

Uig

Orasay Caravan Holiday Home
14 Idrigill, Uig, Isle of Skye,
IV51 9XU
Tel: 01470 542316
Minimum Standard Holiday Caravan

Uig Bay Campsite
10 Idrigill, Uig, Isle of Skye,
IV51 9XU
Tel: 01470 542714
★★★ Touring Park

Kinlochleven

All Seasons Camping & Cabins
MacDonald Hotel, Fort William Road, Kinlochleven, Argyll,
PH50 4QL
Tel: 01855 831539
★★★ Camping Park

Caolasnacon Caravan and Camping Park
Kinlochleven, Argyll, PH50 4RJ
Tel: 01855 831279
★★★ Holiday Park

Onich, by Fort William

Bunree Caravan Club Site
Onich, Fort William, Highland,
PH33 6SE
Tel: 01855 821283
★★★★★ Touring Park

Highland Croft
Onich, Fort William, PH33 6SD
Tel: 01855 821557
Awaiting Inspection

Roy Bridge

Bunroy Camping and Caravaning Site
Roy Bridge, Inverness-shire,
PH31 4AG
Tel: 01397 712332
★★★★ Touring Park

Spean Bridge

Gairlochy Holiday Park
Old Station, Gairlochy Road,
Spean Bridge,
Inverness-shire, PH34 4EQ
Tel: 01397 712711
★★★★ Holiday Park

by Spean Bridge

2 Balmaglaster
by Spean Bridge,
Inverness-shire, PH34 4EB
Tel: 01809 501289
Minimum Standard Holiday Caravan

Strathcarron

Applecross Campsite
Applecross, Strathcarron,
Ross-Shire, IV54 8ND
Tel: 01520 744268
★★★ Touring Park

AVIEMORE AND THE CAIRNGORMS

Aviemore

Dalraddy Holiday Park
Aviemore, Inverness-shire,
PH22 1QB
Tel: 01479 810330
★★★★ Holiday Park

Glenmore Caravan & Camping Site
Glenmore, Aviemore,
Inverness-shire, PH22 1QU
Tel: 01479 861271
★★★ Touring Park

Speyside Highland Leisure Park
Aviemore, PH22 1PX
Minimum Standard Holiday Caravan

Speyside Leisure Park
Dalfaber Road, Aviemore,
Inverness-shire, PH22 1PX
Tel: 01479 810236
★★★★ Holiday Park

Boat of Garten

Boat of Garten Holiday Park
Desmar Road, Boat of Garten,
PH24 3BN
Tel: 01479 831652
★★★★ Holiday Park

Loch Garten Caravan Park
Loch Garten Road,
Boat of Garten,
Inverness-shire, PH24 3BY
Tel: 01479 831769
★★★★ Holiday Park

Grantown-on-Spey

Grantown on Spey Caravan Park
Seafield Avenue,
Grantown on Spey,
Morayshire, PH26 3JQ
Tel: 01479 872474
★★★★★ Holiday Park

Newtonmore

Invernahavon Caravan Site
Glentruim, Newtonmore,
Inverness-shire, PH20 1BE
Tel: 01540 673534
★★★ Touring Park

THE OUTER ISLANDS:
Outer Hebrides, Orkney, Shetland

OUTER HEBRIDES

Drinishader
Minch View Campsite
10 Drinishader, Isle of Harris,
HS3 3DX
Tel: 01859 511207
★★ **Touring Park**

Isle of Benbecula

Liniclate
**Shellbay Caravan &
Camping Park**
Liniclate, Isle of Benbecula,
HS7 5PJ
Tel: 01870 602447
★★ **Touring Park**

Isle of Harris

Grosebay, by Tarbert
5 Grosebay
Grosebay, Isle of Harris,
HS3 3EF
**Minimum Standard Holiday
Caravan**

North Shawbost
Eilean Fraoich Camp Site
North Shawbost, Isle of Lewis,
HS2 9BQ
Tel: 01851 710504
★★★ **Touring Park**

Isle of Lewis

Barvas
Lasgair
3D35 Lower Barvas,
Lower Barvas, Isle of Lewis,
HS2 0QY
Tel: 01851 840409
Awaiting Inspection

Laxdale
Laxdale Holiday Park
6 Laxdale Lane, Laxdale,
Isle of Lewis, HS2 0DR
Tel: 01851 706966
★★★★ **Touring Park**

Isle of Uist

Knockqueen, by Carinish
4 Knockqueen
North Uist, Western Isles,
HS6 5HW
Tel: 01876 580608
**Minimum Standard Holiday
Caravan**

Iochdar
Anglers Retreat
1 Ardmore, Iochdar,
South Uist, HS8 5QY
Tel: 01870 610325
**Minimum Standard Holiday
Caravan**

Lochboisdale
Kilpheder
289 Kilpheder, Lochboisdale,
South Uist, HS8 5TB
Tel: 01878 700425
**Minimum Standard Holiday
Caravan**

Lochside Cottage
Lochboisdale, South Uist,
HS8 5TH
**Minimum Standard Holiday
Caravan**

Ocean View
410 Smerclate, Lochboisdale,
Isle of South Uist, HS8 5TU
Tel: 01878 700383
**Minimum Standard Holiday
Caravan**

Stoneybridge
Crossroads
Stoneybridge, South Uist,
Western Isles, HS8 5SD
**Minimum Standard Holiday
Caravan**

ORKNEY

Kirkwall
**The Pickaquoy Centre
Caravan Park**
Pickaquoy Road, Kirkwall,
Orkney, KW15 1JG
Tel: 01856 879900
★★★ **Touring Park**

Sandwick
Bryameadow Farm
Twatt, Orkney, KW17 2JH
Tel: 01856 841803
**Minimum Standard Holiday
Caravan**

Stromness
Brownstown House
Stromness, Orkney,
KW16 3JN
Tel: 01856 851234
**Minimum Standard Holiday
Caravan**

**Point of Ness Caravan &
Camping Site**
Point of Ness, South End,
Stromness, Orkney, KW16
Tel: 01856 873535
★★★ **Touring Park**

SHETLAND

Eshaness
**Braewick Cafe & Caravan
Park**
Braewick, Eshaness,
Shetland, ZE2 9RS
Tel: 01806 503345
★★★★ **Touring Park**

Lerwick
**Clickimin Caravan &
Camping Site**
Lochside, Lerwick,
Shetland Isles, ZE1 0PJ
Tel: 01595 741000
★★★★★ **Touring Park**

**Skeld Caravan & Camping
Site**
Skeld Waterfront, Skeld,
Shetland, ZE2 9NL
Tel: 01595 860287
Awaiting Inspection

INDEX BY LOCATION

THE NO.1 BOOKING AND INFORMATION SERVICE FOR SCOTLAND   0845 22 55 121   visitscotland.com

THE NO.1 BOOKING AND INFORMATION SERVICE FOR SCOTLAND   0845 22 55 121   visitscotland.com